THE NEW MOVEMENT
IN THE THEATRE

# A STUDENT PRODUCTION OF "AJAX" IN THE GREEK THEATRE, UNIVERSITY OF CALIFORNIA

*This picture might well provide a text for the entire book. In the first place it shows a theatre that was built in the right spirit, preserving all the beauty and dignity of its Greek models, but without slavish archæological exactness, and yet without regard to the false limitations of modern "stage art." Then there is the simple, almost bare, setting; it shows that the producers realized that real drama is independent of the artificial "scenery" and crowded naturalistic "properties" that clutter up the commercial theatre stages. In the grouping of the figures, too, there is a fine sense of design, of decoration, a realization of the effectiveness of purely visual beauty; and in the actors themselves a refreshing virginal beauty that is almost unknown in the usual sophisticated American theatre. And above all there is the fact that something new is being done, that these people are breaking away from the dry conventions, the accepted limitations of the older theatre.*

*All these things bespeak change, progress, a breaking from tradition, a brave independence of thought and deed, a reaching backward and forward to the real essential beauties of dramatic art. And that is what this book is about: chiefly about the breaking away from tradition, and the spirit of change; about the passing from the theatre of artificiality and a false naturalism, and the coming of sincerity and design and decoration. It is a book of living changes, and not of dead periods; a book of the present and future, and not of the past.*

# THE NEW MOVEMENT
# IN THE THEATRE

BY
SHELDON CHENEY

GREENWOOD PRESS, PUBLISHERS
WESTPORT, CONNECTICUT

Originally published in 1914
by Mitchell Kennerley, New York

First Greenwood Reprinting 1971

Library of Congress Catalogue Card Number 70-95089

SBN 8371-3081-6

Printed in the United States of America

But.
Sen.
974

## ˙PREFATORY NOTE

I have a certain respect for authority, but very
little respect for what is commonly taken (like medi-
cine) as authoritative criticism.   If a point of view
has been established in writing these essays, it is
that of the student.   The "authority" necessarily
judges by set standards, and when vital changes come
he is all at sea; whereas the student is free to seek
gold where he will.   Thus I have sifted the sands
of many a new current—and here the resulting treas-
ures are offered to him who has patience to read.
If the authority complain that the offerings have not
the sanction of time, I may only retort that I believe
the over-enthusiastic student is a better guide than
the over-cautious critic.   Nothing has been put down
here in haste or without thought.   If my judgments
still fail—if I seem too tolerant toward the things
that are new—it must be because futurism appeals to
me more than archæology as a force for progress
in art.   In writing of the arts of the theatre I would
rather be a futurist than an archivist.

Of the essays that are collected in this volume

3

three are now published for the first time. The others have appeared in *The Theatre* and *The Forum;* and to the editors of these magazines I am indebted for permission to reprint. Although all of the essays have been rewritten, to shape them into a definite sequence and to bring out the continuity of thought, still each one has been kept complete in itself, even at the risk of repetition.

Since I was writing of a contemporary movement, most of the material came from the theatre itself, or, failing that, from newspaper and magazine reviews. Still I wish to acknowledge a general obligation to three books: Gordon Craig's *On the Art of the Theatre,* Jacques Rouché's *L'Art Theatral Moderne,* and Huntly Carter's *The New Spirit in Drama and Art.* I have felt that the best expression of my gratitude to the several artists of the theatre who have put material at my disposal, would be to treat the work of each justly in the essays themselves— and this I have done as far as my ability served.

S. C.

# CONTENTS

PREFATORY NOTE
*Page 3*

CHAPTER I

THE NEW MOVEMENT IN THE THEATRE
*Page 13*

Conditions Preceding the New Movement—What It Is—
Some of Its Prophets—The Three Expressions of the Movement—Re-theatralizing the Drama—A Protest Against Naturalism—Psychological Drama—The School of Sincerity—
Its Leaders—The New Movement in America.

CHAPTER II

THE ÆSTHETIC THEATRE MOVEMENT
*Page 45*

The Theatre "a Place for Seeing"—Why the Æsthetic
Drama Is the Truest Art of the Theatre—Gordon Craig—
His Theatre of Marionettes—Max Reinhardt and the
Mimo-drama—Sumurun—Leo Bakst and the Dance-
Drama.

CHAPTER III

THE NEW ENGLISH DRAMATISTS
*Page 67*

Psychological Drama on the Continent—The Creed of the
English School—John Galsworthy and His Plays—Ber-

5

nard Shaw—Other Important Playwrights of To-day and
To-morrow.

CHAPTER IV

THE AMERICAN PLAYWRIGHT AND THE DRAMA OF
SINCERITY

*Page 91*

The Tendency of the American Playwright—His Shortcomings—Their Causes—Percy MacKaye, Josephine Preston Peabody, and the Poetic Drama—MacKaye's Antithesis, Eugene Walter—Other Representative Playwrights and
Their Work.

CHAPTER V

THE NEW STAGE-CRAFT

*Page 121*

Staging in Its Relation to the Production as a Whole—The
Fundamentals of the New Stage-craft—How They Are
Attained—Examples of the Old and New School—Certain
Architectural Details—Practitioners of the New Stage-craft
—Gordon Craig and the Germans.

CHAPTER VI

THE FAILURE OF THE AMERICAN PRODUCER

*Page 151*

The Realization of a False Ideal—David Belasco—His
Theory—His Practice—Lavishness and Realism—Their Effect on the Audience—The Boston Toy Theatre—The Chicago Little Theatre—Other Followers of the New Stage-
craft in America.

Chapter VII

THE REAL PROGRESS OF THE AMERICAN THEATRE

*Page 177*

The Experimental Theatre versus Commercialism—The Art Theatre in Chicago, Boston, and New York—Drama in the Universities—Harvard, the Dramatic Workshop—The University of California and Its Revivals—Activities Elsewhere —Effect of the Experimental Theatre on Broadway—The Open Air Theatre—Its Limitations—The Greek Theatre of the University of California—The Open Air Theatre a Factor Toward Greater Democracy.

Chapter VIII

SOME THOUGHTS ON THEATRE ARCHITECTURE

*Page 207*

Present Theatre Construction and Decoration—The Theatre Should Be a Temple of Art—Certain Things an Architect Should Have in Mind—Modern Stage-craft as It Affects Theatre Construction—Scenery, Revolving Stage, etc.—Fortuny Lighting—Professor Max Littmann.

Chapter IX

ON APPLAUSE IN THE THEATRE

*Page 231*

A Useless Disturbance—Actors on Applause—A Plea for Silence.

### Chapter X

#### A NEW THEORY OF THE THEATRE

*Page 243*

Original Meaning of the Words: "Theatre," "Drama"—The Difference Between Them—Various Activities of the Theatre—The Æsthetic Drama—The Drama of Emotion—The Drama of Thought—Definition of Some of the Terms Used.

### Chapter XI

#### GORDON CRAIG'S SERVICE TO THE THEATRE

*Page 275*

Gordon Craig, Innovator—His Point of Departure—His Creed—His Fitness for His Work—The Puppet-theatre—the Mimo-drama—Craig's Influence on the Staging of Modern Psychological Plays—Certain Misconceptions Dispelled—What the Theatre Owes to Gordon Craig.

# ILLUSTRATIONS

FACING
PAGE

A Student Production of "Ajax" in the Greek
Theatre, University of California   *Frontispiece*

Scene from "Twelfth Night," as Produced by
Granville Barker                                      32

The Palace Exterior in "Sumurun"                      48

The Adoration of the Shepherds                        58

The New Adaptable Settings                           106

Max Reinhart's Production of "Hamlet"                130

The New Stage-Craft                                  140

A Belasco Setting                                    154

An Awful Example                                     164

A Christmas Pantomime at the Chicago Little
Theatre                                              186

The Greek Theatre at the University of California                                               196

The Greek Theatre at Point Loma                      202

The Munich Art Theatre                               212

The Little Theatre, New York                         222

An Opera Setting by Joseph Urban                     256

Gordon Craig's Screen Settings                       290

9

# I

## THE NEW MOVEMENT IN THE THEATRE

# THE NEW MOVEMENT IN THE THEATRE

## I

When the peoples of the earth entered upon the present period of progress, reconsidering the old standards and traditions in every other activity of life, they curiously neglected the theatre. Looking back in dramatic history only a very few years, one may see a condition of stagnation unstirred by any dissatisfaction with old forms, and untroubled by any thought for the demands of art. Even the traditions of the church were challenged before those of the playhouse.

But in a very few years the new movement in the theatre has germinated and budded, so that to-day there is very definite promise of such a flowering as the drama has not known since the days of Queen Elizabeth. In remarkable strides the theatre is catching up with life, and—it is quite as important, though generally forgotten—with art. Within a decade there has been infused into the old body

13

more new blood than for three centuries before.

The new spirit that has come into the dramatic world is the spirit of change—of experiment. It is the spirit of dissatisfaction with traditional forms, which has entered not only into the arts but into every activity of civilization. The men and women of the world are busy breaking down the prejudices of the centuries in religion, in economics, in art. They are busy, too, creating new standards of religious and economic conduct that are more just and more free than the old, and creating new forms of art that are less cramped and more beautiful than those the world heretofore has known.

The remarkable expansion of the dramatic arts is merely a reflection of humanity's desire and effort for fuller living, fuller experience, and fuller expression. It is a part of the pushing-out in all directions that is termed modern human progress.

When such widely antithetical figures as Gordon Craig and John Galsworthy, as Max Reinhardt and Brieux, are among the leaders of the movement in the theatre, it is not remarkable that there is much confusion concerning it in the minds of drama-lovers. The development is in such widely diversified directions, and it is so much a reflection of the life of change which all of us are living to-day, that impersonal judgment is exceedingly difficult, and an adequate summary of the movement almost impossible. But now, without being able to catalogue and

pigeon-hole the many artists and productions concerned, the close observer still may note two well-
defined general trends of progress.  Through the
many changes in form and treatment, two very distinct new notes are struck.

The breaking down of the old theory and the
old rules has come in two ways:  first through the
attempt to reach back to an art that is typically
theatric, and at the same time purely æsthetic; and
second through the attempt to develop the existing
drama to a form more typically dramatic, and at the
same time social and indirectly intellectual.

The old theory of the theatre made no distinction
between what was typically theatric and what was
typically dramatic.  The new artists of the theatre
not only make that distinction, but are pushing their
experiments as far as possible to each extreme.  Thus
the first significant current of progress is in the development of an art of the theatre that is visual and
decorative and that appeals primarily to the outward senses; whereas the second significant achievement is in the development of an intensive drama
dependent upon character-development and development of idea through story, and appealing to the
emotions and intellect.

The one new form is the *æsthetic drama:* a typical
theatric art that is as far as possible removed from
the emotional and intellectual elements, tending to
become purely sensuous.  The other new form is

the intensive *drama of emotion and thought:* a drama divorced as far as possible from visual and sensuous appeals, affording deep emotional experience and intellectual stimulus. In studying these two extreme types one may find a third significant development where the two currents touch, where the æsthetic theatre movement and the intensive drama movement border and fuse. This third development may be called the *re-theatralizing* of the drama; it is the attempt to bring all the arts of the theatre into more perfect relation with the limitations of the playhouse; and to invent a stage-craft that will serve to mount beautifully the plays of either the æsthetic or psychologic type.

Both of the extreme new forms are protests against the latter-day stagnation of the theatre. Both are revolts from artificial conventions and traditional standards. But while one, the drama of thought, is a new building on the old dramatic foundations, the other, the æsthetic theatre, is a new creation from the ground up, a form diametrically opposite to the accepted dramatic productions in its very conception of the first principles of theatre art. The term "the new art of the theatre" usually has been applied to the æsthetic drama, rather than to the drama of thought; and when one speaks of the secessionists from the regular theatre, or of the revolutionists, the names that come to mind are Gordon Craig and Max Reinhardt and Leon Bakst, rather

than Ibsen, Shaw, Galsworthy and Brieux.  Because
the Craig-Bakst development is more clearly an absolute revolt, it is the better point of attack in considering the whole movement.

## II

The inception of the æsthetic theatre came perhaps twenty years ago as a reaction from the current
cut-and-dried form of play.  A few enthusiasts realized that the contemporary production in the theatre
was without artistic unity, ranging from mere banal-
ity on the one hand to a conscious didacticism on the
other, but seldom touching within the realms of art.
If there was an "advanced drama" movement, it
was merely an attempt to make the theatre an inter-
preter of undramatic literature.  The visionaries, as
men termed them, dreamed of an art of the theatre
that would be true to the underlying principles of
all art, imaginative, creative, and unified, and at the
same time true to the visual element implied in the
word "theatre."  Out of their dreams have come the
several developments which together make up the
æsthetic theatre: the marionette dramas of Gordon
Craig; the mimo-dramas of Craig and Max Reinhardt; the dance-dramas; and, less directly, the revival of pageantry.

The æsthetic theatre movement as a whole bears

to the regular theatre the relationship of Impressionism to all painting; in its appeal to the senses, it is
to all drama what Swinburne's musical verse is to
literature.  In æsthetics, it is on that side of the
dramatic field which borders on music.  It is conventional and impressionistic, rather than realistic.
Instead of relying chiefly upon theme or story, which
kindle the emotions through subtleties of thought
conveyed in words, this new form makes its sensuous
appeal to eye and ear—mainly through pure beauty
of sight and sound.  Its essence is action in the visual
sense: physical movement rather than story-development.  In subject-matter it is necessarily removed
from the present; it is the revelation of imagination,
rather than the reflection of life; to merely imitate
life, its followers argue, is not artistic creation.  In
order that the appeal to the senses may be simple
and suggestive, creating sustained mood, it affords
perfect unity and harmony of component parts, as,
for instance, of action, music and setting.

Gordon Craig first advanced the principles of an
æsthetic theatre in print, and first applied them to
practical production.  It is worth while to trace his
development in some detail, more than that of any
other leader of the æsthetic movement.

When Gordon Craig came into the theatre as director of staging, he brought with him knowledge
gained from the double training as actor and decorative artist.  Knowing the principles of art, he recog-

nized the almost total lack of art in his own profession.  He expressed the then revolutionary conviction that there were living no true artists of the
theatre.  In order that the dramatic production
may be a thing of unity and harmony, he argued,
there must be one creative mind directing throughout,
a mind capable of conceiving and writing the play
or scenario, of designing the setting and lighting and
costuming, and of training the actors.  Only in this
way can the production be a thing of prevision, and
of definite design.  Any artistic ensemble would be
spoiled when left undirected to the confused invention of playwright, manager, scene painter, carpenter, actor, and the hundred others concerned in the
average theatre "show."

Studying all the elements of dramatic art, in their
entirety, as no man ever had studied them before,
Gordon Craig deduced certain principles that he
believed should govern all the arts of the theatre.
In general they are the principles that underlie every
later development of the æsthetic theatre.  As here
summarized, they may be considered as fairly expressive of the ideals of the entire movement, though
certain departures and differing emphasis will be
noted in the several individual forms.

In the first place the whole production must be
woven into a single fabric, conceived and executed in
unity and harmony—implying in the artist an understanding of every department of theatre work, and

the ability to synthesize all the elements. In order that the resultant mood may be sustained, the drama must be stripped of every unnecessary detail of story and of setting: thus the attention will not be distracted from the spiritual and imaginative essence of the production to those things which are of interest in themselves but contribute nothing to the main design. Archæological accuracy in detail of setting, and historical truth in story, may be entirely disregarded, as long as the production carries to the spectator the more intangible sense of beauty of atmosphere and artistic truth. In the selection of material the accidentally striking and the photographically correct will give way to that which is characteristically beautiful. The imaginative story must be neither immoral nor consciously moral; simply unmoral. The setting must be decorative but unobtrusive, and must in color and form strike the keynote of the production; the "scenery" should serve merely as a harmonious background for the action, and not, by any striking beauty of its own, draw attention to itself. The lighting should be beautiful rather than imitative of nature, and should serve to heighten the atmospheric illusion. The costumes should be part of the decorative scheme in color and design. In order that the actors may become part of the harmonious whole, they must realize the value of directed movement, and give up the inartistic attempt to appear "natural" through individual tricks

and "realistic" restlessness.  Rhythm of line and
form should make the movement and grouping of
the actors a very valuable decorative feature.  In
fact, decorative movement should be of the very essence of the production.

In following out these more general principles of
dramatic production to their logical conclusion, Gordon Craig developed a particular form of theatre
art, the silent drama of marionettes.  When he came
to the conclusion that the production must be the
work of one man, he started to simplify by discarding every unnecessary member of the producing staff;
he was able to eliminate scene painter, costume
designer, and stage manager, by himself designing the settings, costumes and action, and personally
directing their execution.  But it was impossible for
him personally to do the work of the actors.  But
living actors, with emotions of their own, he argued,
cannot subordinate themselves to the will of the director to the extent of obeying him absolutely in
movement and expression; and the director must
work only in materials yielding an absolute response
to his own impulses.  There was only one thing to
do: abolish the actor, and find an absolutely responsive substitute.  He substituted the "super-marionette."  The change necessitated a drama of silence; but far from being distressed by this limitation, Gordon Craig found it to be an advantage;
for, he argued, the strong feelings of primitive and

imaginative stories can be expressed better by gestures than by words. So there came into being the first form of æsthetic drama, an art of silent marionettes acting a simple and elemental story, appealing to the senses by the harmony and rhythm and sensuous beauty of perfectly blended movement, lighting and setting.

Though one of the first forms to be evolved from the new conception of theatre art, and though more closely approximating the impersonal sensuous ideal than any other, the new marionette drama still remains to some extent an unproved form. It is one of the three or four very significant phases of the new æsthetic art, but Gordon Craig and his fellow-artists have worked under such handicaps of imperfect equipment and limited resources that the marionette theatre is yet to come to its full perfection. It has shown the possibility, and even the probability, of taking a very important place among the theatre arts; but its effectiveness is in some measure provisional until it becomes less an art of the few.

To Gordon Craig must be given the credit for recreating the art of pantomime, that in its new and more artistic form has been rechristened the "mimodrama." But while Craig undoubtedly paved the way for the perfection of this second of the forms of æsthetic drama, it is no less true that Max Reinhardt has carried it farthest along the road to that perfection.

Professor Reinhardt has been practically and commercially more successful than any other artist of the æsthetic theatre movement. Instead of working slowly and patiently, bringing forth with infinite pains a very few plays, and those only for a very select audience, he has put on the stage in a few years a remarkably large number of surprisingly varied productions. Necessarily some were uninteresting, some were bizarre, and many were only imperfectly expressive of the new ideals. Thus Professor Reinhardt gained the name of "realist-symbolist," with the implied contradiction of material and method. Nevertheless "The Miracle" and "Sumurun," produced under his direction, are the most typical examples of the mimo-drama that have been given to the world. "Sumurun" was one of the few actual dramas of the æsthetic theatre produced in America. It had touches of a bizarre sort of realism, and of sensationalism, that were Reinhardt's personal additions to the new ideas; nevertheless it was very typical of the whole æsthetic theatre in its wordless presentation of the story, in its dependence upon sensuous beauty of component parts, and in its flat neutrally-toned settings, which often were mere hangings. Altogether Reinhardt has been more instrumental than any other artist of the theatre in forcing a general acceptance of the underlying principles of the æsthetic drama. Certainly the mimo-drama as he has developed it is the most widely recognized of all the activities of the æsthetic theatre.

There is more than mere coincidence in the parallel between the growth of the æsthetic theatre and the revival of pageantry. The pageant was one of the earliest expressions of man's dramatic instinct, and its growth to artistic proportions is no new development, to be credited to any late phase of theatre expansion. Accurately speaking, the pageant is not of the theatre. But in its way of appeal it distinctly is allied with the forms of art that Gordon Craig and Max Reinhardt have developed. And its recent achievement of a long-lost splendor, and particularly its occasional accomplishment of a purely æsthetic ideal, shadow forth clearly the debt it owes to the new arts of the theatre. When least concerned with literary or historical subject, and most dependent upon the movement of decorative masses of figures, and upon the beauty of dancing and costumes and setting, the pageant may well be considered a worthy form of mimo-drama, deserving a distinct place in the new alignment of the dramatic arts.

Of all the arts of the theatre, the "dance-drama" is farthest removed from the literary or psychologic drama. It is the form of æsthetic drama that most completely subordinates subject-interest to beauty of expression. In its most notable type, the Russian Ballet, it approaches music in the pure sensuousness of its appeal. Like opera, it is in some measure a bastard form, calling in music as one of its elements; but it is more truly an art of the theatre because the visual remains the dominant appeal. The dance-drama is like the arts of Craig and Reinhardt in its first principles of unity and harmony: but the synthesis here is one of dancing, music, and decorative and colorful setting. The stage-setting, instead of remaining a mere neutral background, becomes one of the three very important sources of compelling beauty; and the blended beauty of movement, sound and scenic decoration appeals simultaneously to the eye and ear. The Russian Ballet has brought the painter-decorator into the theatre, and has given to such artists as Leon Bakst an opportunity to paint gorgeous stage-pictures in terms of miles of canvas and great masses of moving figures. Moreover it has brought back the poetry of dancing from its temporary exile.

Such are the easily distinguished forms of the æsthetic drama: the marionette play; the mimo-drama; the re-created pageant; and the dance-drama. If the movement brought forth no other forms, or no other phases than those described, it still would be notable as one of the great creative developments of theatre art. And yet there are other less definitely developed types, other phases which so closely shade into those enumerated that it is difficult to differentiate them. Thus there is a certain sort of poetic drama that has been staged with the visual and æsthetic appeals emphasized; there are certain forms of spectacle that have been almost divorced from the distracting episodic action and the distracting pursuit of naturalism that so commonly degrade spectacle; and there is the so-called "relief-drama." These phases may well carry us over to the consideration of the middle ground, to that development where the æsthetic theatre fuses with the new intensive psychologic drama: to the movement that has been termed the "re-theatralizing of the drama."

## III

The re-theatralizing of the drama may be described as the attempt to perfect the visual side of plays that are typically dramatic, that is, that are dependent upon the sustained appeal of uninterrupted action: the attempt to fit more perfectly to the theatre the forms of drama that are least theatric. It has resulted in the creation of a new stage-craft that permits the mounting of plays of every kind in beautiful style, without drawing the spectator's attention from the story-development; and it has brought about a total discrediting of the naturalistic method of theatre production. The new stage-craftsmen have "theatralized" many an old drama that formerly had nothing but a literary appeal; or that perhaps had served in the theatre merely as a centre around which an enterprising producer built all sorts of naturalistic "effects." They have brought every sort of drama into proper relationship with the playhouse, accentuating the purely decorative or visual elements when possible, but always fitting the method of setting to the spirit of the play.

The truth is that the principles of setting that Gordon Craig and his followers have worked out are those which should apply to every production in the theatre, whether aimed to appeal primarily to the senses, like the æsthetic drama, or not. That the setting of the drama should be beautiful or tasteful in itself, that it should be in harmony with the essential spirit of the production, or even strike a keynote for the whole production, and that it should be unobtrusive and so designed as not to distract attention from the more important action, are principles that seem obvious enough now that Craig has stated them. But they were practically never applied to staging until he came into the theatre. Now, however, there is a very definite movement toward their acceptance, and against the naturalism which David Belasco in America, and Sir Herbert Tree in England, have so exploited.

The artists of the new movement have shown that even the simplest hangings, with their long lines and restful masses, are more fitted to be the background of the average drama than the usual tawdry flapping

scenery.  They have pointed out the impossibility of
making painted perspective look right from more
than one point in the auditorium, and the inevitable
discrepancy between the painted and the actual
shadows; and they have shown how each superfluous
object on the stage tends to draw the eye away from
the action.  Now even those producers who are
farthest removed from the ideals of the æsthetic
theatre are recognizing that the acceptance of these
principles is less a fad than a return to the foundations which underlie all true dramatic art.

Gordon Craig has perfected a new system of
screen settings, which are easily shifted, thus doing
away with the necessity of long waits between the
acts; which do not interfere with lighting from the
top and sides, thus allowing the inartistic footlight
to be eliminated; and which provide a neutral and
harmonious background for the action.  Using these
screens as the setting for the so-called poetic or
literary drama, Craig has achieved much the same
success in harmonizing action, lighting and setting
as in the pure æsthetic drama.  His production of
"Hamlet" at the Moscow Art Theatre, with no other
background than a series of folding cream-colored
screens, shifted into differing combinations and
bathed in varying lights to afford the proper atmospheric moods, was remarked by discerning critics
as bringing a new significance to Shakespeare in the
theatre.

When Max Reinhardt "theatralizes" a play he is likely to strain it out of all semblance to its original self.  Where Craig is jealous to preserve all that the original dramatist intended, conceiving this part of his theatre work as merely interpretative, Reinhardt produces something typically Reinhardtian though usually reminiscent of the thing with which he started.  Thus he metamorphosed "Œdipus Rex" into a production startlingly effective, but hardly true to the spirit of the play or to the best ideals of dramatic art.  But Reinhardt has at times been one of the most successful of those who attempt to stage the masterpieces of drama according to the new conception of theatre art.  He probably has directed more productions in which the stage-art perfectly fitted the play than any other man of the theatre. Both Max Reinhardt and George Fuchs had much to do with the development of the "relief-theatre," where the aim is to accentuate the decorative value of the moving figures, by the use of a very shallow stage and a very flat background.  On the relief-stage the actors stand out almost exactly like statues on a bas-relief panel.

In Germany there are many theatres where the drama is being produced with the literary element subordinated as far as possible and the more truly theatric elements emphasized.  In no other country have the theatres such adequate equipment, and in no other country are there so many directors and designers who understand the principles of the new stage-craft—and, parenthetically, nowhere else has the new art been carried to such bizarre and sensational extremes. But there are leaders elsewhere: Constantin Stanislavsky in Russia, Alexander Hevesi in Hungary, Jacques Rouché in France. These men are working continually toward the simplification and the unification of the whole fabric of the drama. They are teaching that the scenic background may be decorative and yet harmonious and unobtrusive; and they are carrying on the fine battle against naturalism in stage setting. Even in England, that dealt so impatiently with Gordon Craig's new ideas, there recently have been productions in the new style, under the direction of Granville Barker; and in America there are the first stirrings of a new theatre conscience.

## IV

There is a curious intolerance in the attitude of the followers of the æsthetic theatre toward the psychologic or intensive drama, and often an unfortunate impatience among the followers of the latter art toward the former. Probably the cause is to be found in that the followers of the one form continually visualize the other in its imperfections, while they are able, through long poring over their own type, to see it in its ultimate ideal beauty. As a matter of fact the æsthetic theatre and the best development of the psychologic are similar in that both are reactions from the old and generally accepted inartistic forms.  While contrasted, both are founded on the principles of art, and are returns to simplicity, unity and truth.  Both are distinctly arts of the theatre, even though one is more typically theatric.  The differences are not in the fundamental art principles, but in the authors' aims, and in their emphasis on material.  To say that the lover of drama cannot appreciate the one form and remain true to the other, is like saying that one cannot appreciate both painting and sculpture, or that one cannot recognize the richly delicate beauty of an etching and still feel the charm of a Japanese print.

"Psychologic drama" is a term coined to identify all those forms of drama which appeal primarily to the emotions and intellect, as distinguished from the æsthetic drama, which appeals primarily to the senses.  The psychologic drama is the more typically dramatic art of the theatre, the æsthetic drama the more typically theatric.  Where the latter appeals by outward charm of movement, lighting, color, and sound, the former appeals by the subtle development of a story of human souls.  The psychologic drama is the drama of soul-crises; it is the drama that grips the emotions, that compels the spectator in effect to live through the events the dramatist has chosen to bring to the stage.

The psychologic drama includes more than the development that is the second significant current of the new movement in the theatre. It includes both the drama of emotion, that exists entirely for emotional story-development, and the drama of thought, that reaches through the emotions to the intellect. The drama of thought is the new intensive drama, that, like the æsthetic drama, is typically a growth of the current period of progress.

When Ibsen, the father of the modern drama of thought, brought forth his first compact, intensive social dramas, the western theatre had been abandoned to the shallow inventions of the Scribe-Sardou school of playwrights. The drama of emotion had become hardly more than a hollow shell: a cut-and-dried formula by which clever men could put on the stage type characters and stock situations that would trick the audience into an unthinking emotional response. Sincerity, poetry, thought, had gone out of the theatre. It is the achievement of the dramatists of the new movement, from the pioneer Ibsen to Shaw and Galsworthy, that the drama of emotion has been made again into a thing of sincerity, touched with poetic beauty, and finally raised to a drama of thought by an added intellectual and social significance. The old dry form has been made over until it yields a true emotional appeal, and, over and above that, a distinct intellectual stimulus.

While the drama of thought flowered first in the

SCENE FROM "TWELFTH NIGHT"
AS PRODUCED BY GRANVILLE BARKER

*With the exception of one feature this is an excellent setting, and in accord with the newest ideas of stage-craft. The flat-toned, conventionally designed background throws all the emphasis on the actors. The one bizarre note is in the design of the trees. These are over-conventionalized to the point of absurdity, and by drawing attention to themselves defeat the artists' effort to render the total setting unobtrusive. Cover the two trees with pieces of paper, and then note how decoratively the figures stand out, and how fine the scene is from the standpoint of pictorial composition.*

*(By courtesy of the Daily Mirror Studios, London.)*

Northern Countries it has been a definite world movement, felt sooner or later in England and in Russia, in Japan and in Germany, in America, in Italy, in France, in Spain. In Scandinavia there came and went the wonderful trio, Ibsen, Strindberg and Björnson; in Russia, for a brief space, the giant Tolstoy, and after him Gorky and Tchekhoff; in Germany Hauptmann and Sudermann, and the more powerful but less temperate Wedekind; the Italian Giacosa, and the French Brieux; and finally the most notable of all contemporary groups: the Englishmen, Shaw, Barker, Galsworthy, and those others who join with them in what is called the Modern English School.

It is with the English School that we may most profitably concern ourselves here. For the English dramatists are the greatest in achievement and the greatest in promise of all the groups existing in the dramatic world to-day. In their plays, more typically than in any others, may be traced the development and the final perfection of the drama of thought.

Just as the English dramatists of the late sixteenth century had to break through the shackles of a double limitation of church heredity and a revived classicism, so the English dramatists of the end of the nineteenth had to struggle on the one hand against a prevailing dry convention of thought, and on the other against a cut-and-dried standard

of dramatic entertainment.  They found a public that was willing to look at life only through the
smoked glasses of a conventional prudery; and they
faced in the theatre a set standard of artificiality,
that decreed a happy ending to every play of contemporary story, that relegated tragedy to historic
or purely fanciful subjects, that bound the playwright
in unending and meaningless rules of mechanical
marshalling of his actors, that ruled out everything
that was not sweet and sentimental and conventionally correct, and that made the setting a sort of side-
show, with all kinds of inartistic and distracting
"naturalistic" appeals.

How the English stage returned from all that is
shallow and false to an art of which the very life-
breath is sincerity, is the story of the new English
dramatists.  Without imputing insincerity to the artists of the æsthetic theatre or to any other group,
we may fairly term the new English group "The
School of Sincerity" in playwriting.  For sincerity is
the very keynote of their art.  Above all, their work
rings true.  They are true to life, true to themselves,
and true to art.

In general the drama of sincerity marks a return
from the purely theatrical, which strangled art in
the theatre for so many decades, to the truly dramatic.  It is true to life in the sense of being true to
the deeper motives of human character and to the
underlying currents of social development; not in

the sense of being photographically reflective of
outer aspects and irrelevant details. It does not
strain to appear natural, and yet it never is unnatural. The mirror is not held up to life, but life
is subjected to a rigid selective sense, and through
that transformed to art. The new art of the theatre
differs from the old in depicting the inner spiritual
forces that are dramatic, rather than the chance
happenings that are merely theatrically effective.

The dramatists of thought do not revolt, on the
other hand, from the way of appeal of the old shallow theatre: that is, they address themselves first
to the emotions. They believe that the art of the æsthetic theatre, with its purely sensuous appeal, comes
perilously near to acting merely as an anæsthetic.
They argue that the art which stirs men's souls to
the depths, and leaves food for afterthought, is more
vital than the art which merely touches and lulls
the senses. So they deal in soul-crises, aiming to
make the audience emotionally experience their own
and their characters' feelings. Their productions
are not "problem plays" except in the sense that
everything that concerns the deeper feelings of
thoughtful people is a problem. Because they are
true to their own time, the general spirit of their
plays is humanitarian, or even socialistic in the best
sense of the word; but they are never propagandist.
They have kept their viewpoint as artists of the theatre: so they do not preach, but they make the audi-

ence feel; they remember that true art carries an
intellectual stimulus only through emotional suggestion, and not by direct statement.

Their plays are introspective and intensive.  In
technique they have brought back a compactness of
form that has not been known since the time of the
Greeks.  In subject there are none of the wide
reaches of material and the broad sweeps of time
and place that characterized Elizabethan drama.
Their whole art is intimate and intensive rather
than impersonal and extensive.

The phrase "literary drama" has been applied to
the plays of the intensive dramatists in an attempted
disparagement.  It is really only an added glory.
For no plays ever were written more specifically
for the theatre—or what the theatre ought to be as
a house of art rather than of business—and with
greater regard for the limitations of theatre production.  That Galsworthy's "Strife," and Masefield's "Nan," and Houghton's "Hindle Wakes,"
make very good reading matter, only shows that
the authors are literary artists as well as successful
playwrights; it does not at all show that the plays
are unfitted for stage production.  Those who saw
the unusually fine company which the Manchester
Repertory Theatre sent to America recently in a
series of plays by Galsworthy, Masefield, Arnold
Bennett, and Bernard Shaw, know what keen and
purely dramatic pleasure the dramas of the new

movement afford when interpreted by an adequate
cast of players.

Starting from a "pure art" basis, the æsthetic theatre has enjoyed a certain isolation, which has allowed
it to develop with constant reference to its ideal
form. The drama of thought, on the other hand, has
been close to the accepted theatre, with a consequent
constant temptation to be influenced by old traditions
and commercial standards. The difficult goal which
a few of the newer dramatists have now reached,
doubtless was seen by many who surrendered along
the way. Their failures came chiefly in two general directions: first, in the lowering of standards
by catering to popular taste, as exampled in the con-
scienceless use of improbable happy endings, and in
the introduction of features interesting and sensational in themselves but without organic relation to
the total dramatic design; and second, in the blind
following of schools and masters. A certain group
became convinced that great art lay entirely in the
treatment of the sordid things of life, and they de-
scended to the most depressing intellectual horrors
in their plays. They followed their master, but they
had not his power of so clothing an unpleasant theme
with beauty and spiritual significance that its ultimate form was noble and uplifting. Even now the
dramatists of the new movement are suffering from
a lack of the sense of the nobility of life. They are
not quite close enough to the eternal mysteries of the

wholesome human soul. They too often chill with
a sense of the futility of living, rather than warm
with a sense of the richness of life.

If one is looking for the Shakespeare or the Sophocles of the new movement, it must be admitted
immediately that the time of the great master has
not yet come. The English School has not even
produced a leader who can measure up to its own
forerunners, Ibsen and Strindberg. But it includes
several men who are fairly comparable to Hauptmann and Björnson and Brieux and the other living
Europeans. It is as a group that the school is so
remarkable. For here are half a dozen men who
seem to be young giants dramatically, and as many
more who have produced one or two plays of distinctly lasting quality—and all included in one direction of development in the theatre.

Who, then, are the notable dramatists of this second phase of the revolution in the theatre?

Most typical, and at the same time richest in
promise, is John Galsworthy; for he has developed
most perfectly the drama of second meaning, the
play that at once emotionally purges and inspires to
thought and action; his "Strife" and "The Silver
Box" are among the most powerful productions of
the new movement, and "Justice," while less perfect
dramatically, has proved the social strength of the
new drama. Greatest in stature, but perhaps least
dramatic, is Bernard Shaw: he is the most original

thinker and the most brilliant writer of the group;
but his artistic conscience is defective, and his play
structures often are of the outworn Sardou mould or
cut to no dramatic pattern at all; he is the intellectual and moralistic giant of the school, but he is
not so great an artist as half a dozen of his fellows.
After him comes Granville Barker, with some of the
same faults, and with the same virtues in less remarkable measure; his work often seems a little
pale—doubtless because it so often is placed beside
Shaw's—but he has an originality of his own, and
must be taken into account by any serious historian
of the theatre; in "Waste" and "The Voysey Inheritance" and "The Madras House" he produced typical
dramas of thought.   J. M. Barrie, turning from
literature to the drama, has brought a new literary
distinction to the intensive drama; though at first independent of any group, he lately has exhibited
nearly all the characteristics of the new school.  John
Masefield, though his dramatic work has been very
limited, brought forth "The Tragedy of Nan," that
is as sincere a bit of dramatic writing as has appeared
in England.   Only slightly less important than these
are Arnold Bennett, who never has thrown off completely the novelist's diffuseness, who doubtless has
the ideals of the dramatists of thought but has been
unable to master their economy of means; and the
late St. John Hankin, who saw the light and helped
to break the road for the new school, but had not

the power of Galsworthy and Shaw and Barker.
And there are the dramatists of the Irish School, one
of the most important sub-groups of the new movement; their achievement, from that of the very remarkable prose-poet Synge to that of St. John Ervine, is a triumph of the drama of sincerity. And
in the younger generation are Stanley Houghton,
whose "Hindle Wakes," a play of notable technical
power, independence of thought, and sincerity of
treatment, marked him as a man of great promise;
and Githa Sowerby, who wrote, in "Rutherford and
Son," a taut little drama that had an Ibsen-like simplicity and straightforwardness; and Elizabeth Baker, who wrote "Chains," a promising study of commonplace English life; and Cosmo Hamilton, who,
in "The Blindness of Virtue," wrote a typical idea-
play, but sugared the theme a little too sentimentally.
One might go further afield, and add Israel Zangwill, and Macdonald Hastings, and half a dozen
more, as at least contributory to the movement.
Altogether it is a wonderful array for a single time
and a single place in the history of the theatre.

## V

It only remains to say a word about the progress
of the new movement in the United States. Unfortunately a word will suffice, for the American producer has been concerned with the amusement business rather than with art. In the application of the

principles of the æsthetic theatre, there has been little actual achievement, though one can call to mind several interesting experiments: notably in staging at the Chicago Little Theatre, the Boston Toy Theatre, and the Boston Opera House. At least one artist of the theatre, Livingston Platt, has passed the experimental stage, and directed productions of dignified simplicity and beauty. At the universities, too, there have been notable productions in the truest æsthetic theatre style.

When one considers the psychologic drama and American playwrights, one looks in vain for men to compare with Galsworthy, Shaw, Synge and Houghton. In writing the farce, and in producing the anomalous "play with a punch," there is a great facility on this side of the Atlantic; but there is little of the drama of sincerity, that is at once powerful and subtle, perfect in technique, socially significant, and touched with the magic of poetry. There are poetic playwrights, like the very able Percy Mac-kaye; but they seem not to make their work dramatically persuasive, nor do they reflect the life of the time. On the other hand there are the powerful writers like Eugene Walter and Charles Klein, who often are sincere in that they depict life as they see it; but they lack the sense of beauty; either they have not poets' souls, or they do not put their souls in their work. In the recent American plays there is a great promise and every condition is ripe for its fulfillment.

The material and the audience are ready at hand; they only await the dramatist who is the perfect balance of dramatic craftsman and poet. The actual achievement is small, when one judges by the standard of a Galsworthy; but there are names to conjure with in all seriousness: Mackaye, Knoblauch, Walter, Klein, Augustus Thomas, Broadhurst, Sheldon, Kenyon, Gates.

In summary, one may say that the new movement in America is hardly more than a promise, but that in England and on the Continent it is both a promise and a vital, lasting achievement. The new artists of the theatre have, on the one hand, created an æsthetic theatre, a new form of artistic expression which reveals beauties heretofore undreamed of in connection with the playhouse; on the other hand, they have developed from the regular theatre the new drama of sincerity, replacing the older theatricality with a form that is truly dramatic and socially significant. Indeed, there is a budding of dramatic activity without parallel in the history of the English theatre since the early Elizabethan period; it still is a question whether there will follow the full flower of a second dramatic renaissance; but there are not lacking lovers of the theatre who believe that there will. At least there is no longer a condition of untroubled stagnation in the theatre; and it will be a great many decades before the drama again can be divorced from art.

# II

## THE ÆSTHETIC THEATRE MOVEMENT

# THE ÆSTHETIC THEATRE MOVEMENT

All art is a matter of nature or life acted upon by man; a part taken out of its accidental surroundings and given artistic form. At either side of the field of true art is a waste place, where art ceases to have beauty. And the waste on the one side is reached when the artist becomes so enamored of life that he forgets to interpret, to give artistic form, and only brings forth a photographic image; while the waste on the other side is reached when the artist perfects his form but forgets to put life into it.

When the dreamers of the æsthetic theatre first stepped into the playhouse, the art of the theatre had arrived at both extremes. The drama had been carried to the waste places in both directions, to a naturalism, a false sort of realism, that had nothing to do with art or beauty; and to an artificial form of dramatic structure that was entirely hollow and lifeless. For the men of the theatre were busy, on the one hand, providing new thrills of wonderment at this or that mechanical imitation of nature; and, on the other, pouring into a set mould an unend-

45

ing cycle of type figures and stock situations, as un-like living beings and life as the gas light is unlike the sun.

The æsthetic theatre movement is the most revo-lutionary of the reactions from the condition of stag-nation that pervaded the theatre for the greater part of the nineteenth century. Reaction, even in an institution so bound by tradition as the theatre, was inevitable in the wave of change, of human progress, that swept the world at the end of the century.

The first spirit of life was breathed into the æs-thetic theatre movement on that day when Gordon Craig, after long pondering over the strange things that passed current as the art of the playhouse, took down his dictionary and sought out the word "thea-tre"—and discovered that originally it meant merely "a place for *seeing*." Until one has some faint glimmering of the visions he must have had that day, of the ultimate glorious possibilities of a purely *visual* art of the theatre, one cannot hope to under-stand the æsthetic theatre movement. In the light of his new vision, Gordon Craig re-interpreted the word "action" that appeared in every definition of theatre and drama: for if the word "theatre" stresses seeing as the way of receiving the artistic impression, then the action that is the essence of the art must be of a sort visually effective; that is, see-able action, or *movement;* and not action in the sense of mere story-development or theme-development.

This interpretation of action as movement holds the key to the understanding of the whole development of the æsthetic theatre.   For all the forms of æsthetic drama, the creations alike of Gordon Craig and Max Reinhardt and Leon Bakst, are characteristically visual in appeal.   While Ibsen and Pinero and Galsworthy, and their fellow dramatists of the accepted theatre, have been rearing a very vital form of art upon the foundation of the old interpretation of action, as meaning merely something accomplished, or developed, without regard to beauty of physical movement, their art may be said to be typically dramatic and only incidentally and in small measure theatric; whereas the æsthetic drama is only incidentally dramatic, since the story-development and theme-development are subordinated to visual effectiveness, and is very typically theatric.   Indeed, Gordon Craig is right when he claims that the new æsthetic drama is the truest *art of the theatre;* and the unthinking critics who so impatiently try to wave him aside as mad must reconsider their ground; for all that they really can claim is that the new art is not the truest art *of drama.*

The new conception of the nature of action led to the creation of an art that is different in appeal from any the theatre heretofore has known.   For that which appeals primarily to the eye clearly is sensuous; and the older theatre always appealed primarily to the emotions, or at its best to the emotions and intellect, the outward decorative appeal to the senses being entirely subordinated. The older drama is comparable to that sort of painting in which subject-interest or idea-interest dominates; the æsthetic drama is comparable to the Japanese color-print and the paintings of Whistler, where there is a purely sensuous appeal of beautiful arrangement of line and mass and color. The new drama is a thing of physical beauty, compounded of decorative movement, color and light. In its purest form it has the effect of a gorgeous fluctuating pattern, entrancing the eye and beguiling the mind and emotions to a dreamy forgetfulness. It is the art of the theatre that is most purely æsthetic; it is conventional, imaginative, impressionistic.

Of the two great developments in the modern theatre, one—the intensive social drama, the drama of thought—took root and flowered in the work of one man, Henrik Ibsen; but the other, the æsthetic drama, had first its prophet and then its practitioners. Only by studying together the principles of Gordon Craig and the practice of Max Reinhardt can one learn the best that there is in the æsthetic theatre. For Craig is primarily the creator and seer, Reinhardt the practitioner; Craig the thinker, Reinhardt the doer.

Gordon Craig's first diagnosis of the theatre's trouble was that there were no true artists of the

### THE PALACE EXTERIOR IN "SUMURUN"

*This wordless play, produced by Max Reinhardt, was acted entirely before flat, perspectiveless backgrounds, against which the gorgeously costumed figures stood out conspicuously and decoratively. Look at the scene for a moment, noting how the eye is drawn just where it belongs —to the actors. Then think back to the other Oriental palaces you have seen on the stage: to the mazes of columns and domes, the intricate stucco patterns, the glittering tinsel and gold, the distant painted towers and sky, and the clutter of baskets and vases and rugs in the foreground. You should need no other contrast to accentuate the restfulness, the good taste, and the perfect fitness to purpose of this "Sumurun" palace.*

*(By courtesy of Winthrop Ames.)*

theatre, no men who understood every detail of creation from the playwriting to the costuming and lighting—and consequently there was no unity of structure in the average production, and no harmony of effect. In order to avoid the usual scattered effect, he argued, there must be one all-seeing and all-powerful director. This artist must conceive the production as a whole, and conceive it according to the true principles of theatre art; he must write the play or scenario, design the setting and costumes, and direct the movement of the figures on the stage.

Working from this conception of the complete production as a single art (playwriting, and scene painting, and costume designing existing individually as only provisional or incomplete art), and from the idea of one director having absolute control, Gordon Craig progressed logically to the form of æsthetic drama that is his particular contribution to the practical part of the movement; the drama of the *super-marionette*. The artist of the theatre, he argued, can write the play and design the scenery and costumes, but he cannot take the place of the actors; and yet living actors, with wills and temperaments of their own, never can pass completely under the dominance of the director: he never can control their every impulse and their every movement; and since he must have only the materials that are absolutely responsive, he must work with marionettes, that never will move, or bow to the audience, or blow their noses, without the authority of the master-artist. Automatically the substitution of the wooden figures for actors transformed the new form to a drama of silence. Never mind!—Gordon Craig said —for then it will be a more typical art of the theatre, since there will be no words and no literary interest to interfere with the decorative appeal to the eye. This is not the place to debate the fallacy of the argument as applying to any all-embracing theory of the theatre; and for the moment we may well be content to admit that this silent, dehumanized drama is characterized more than any other by the "noble artificiality" that Craig and many others attribute to the highest forms of art.

When Gordon Craig turned to the marionettes, he found that the art of the puppet theatre had degenerated to a sort of circus entertainment; the jerky Punch-and-Judy shows, with their exaggerated stories and slap-stick humor, were almost all that remained of a department of the theatre that once had been a much-loved and dignified source of pleasure. Craig dreamed of the rejuvenation of the marionette drama in accordance with the new conception of a typically visual art of the theatre. Gradually he and his followers developed the super-marionette, by adding a new beauty and a more perfect responsiveness to the old types. And while perfecting the wooden figures they brought out new beauties in the backgrounds or settings and in the lighting. The resultant art-form, which makes its appeal primarily through the decorative movement of richly dressed puppets in suggestive settings amid changing lights is the super-marionette drama, that recently has brought about the crossing of swords among so many dramatic critics and artists.

Before judging this development of the æsthetic theatre, the average American must rid himself of a false conception of the marionette, gained from the degraded descendants of the true type that are the only examples on this side of the Atlantic. It is difficult for him to realize what a large place the toy theatre holds in the affections of the German child; and that throughout Europe men and women often find the better puppet-shows a source of pleasure quite comparable with the regular theatre. Such discerning writers as Arthur Symons and Anatole France and Maurice Maeterlinck have attested to the exquisite pleasure they have derived from the drama of wooden figures. In the past two or three years there has been a remarkable revival of interest in marionettes, due primarily to the Craig experiments, and innumerable puppet theatres have sprung up throughout Europe. Amateurs and professionals alike are proving the beauty of the new art form, from the mere dilettante to the directors of commercial marionette theatres. One of the best known of the European puppet theatres is the "Marionetten-Theater Münchner Künstler," which is about the size of the Little Theatre in New York. The building is designed exclusively for marionette productions, and performances are given every night during the regular dramatic season. It is interesting to note that Clayton Hamilton, one of the most intelligent of American dramatic critics—who, however, in 1912 had characterized Gordon Craig's ideas as clearly "mad"—visited the Munich Marionette theatre in 1913, and testified that he became so absorbed in the production that he "lost all sense of the puppets as puppets." The acting he described as "less wooden than that of many of our so-called artists." And he added, wisely: "This may lead us to wonder whether Mr. Gordon Craig was quite as insane as many people thought him when he suggested that the drama of the future should be presented not by the ordinary human actor but by a sort of super-puppet that he called by the barbarous name of Über-Marionette. . . . Certain it is that such well-endowed puppets as those of the miniature theatre in Munich are less likely to obscure the original intention of an author than such crude and bungling actors as we often meet with in our theatres."

The puppet theatre is not the most important development of the æsthetic drama movement; nor is it the most valuable phase of Gordon Craig's service to the theatre. For while perfecting the marionette drama, he solved certain problems that pertain to all theatre production, and he promulgated those prin-

ciples that underlie the whole æsthetic movement.
The new conception of the value of movement, and
the new conception of unity of structure and harmony of impression, are the very heart and soul of
all the forms of æsthetic drama; and the principles
of decorative beauty and unobtrusiveness, of simplicity and concentration and suggestion, in stage setting,
apply to almost every production in any department
of the theatre.   It is from this part of Craig's work
rather than from his actual achievement with the
marionettes, that the great æsthetic advance has followed.   While Craig has shown in scattered productions that his practical work includes more than the
marionette drama, he remains in other directions the
great theorist and only the partially effective practitioner; and when we turn to the second development
of the æsthetic theatre, the mimo-drama of living
actors, it is in Max Reinhardt's rather than Craig's
work that we shall find its most typical expression.

"Mimo-drama" is a term which properly applies
to all silent forms of drama; but in its latter-day
use it has been narrowed so that it seldom is meant
to include the marionette drama, but only those
wordless plays whose stories are worked out by flesh-
and-blood actors.   It is the drama that appeals to the
senses by visual beauty of line and mass and color,
and chiefly of moving human figures; that unrolls before the eye a kaleidoscopic decoration, a fluctuating
pattern of sinuous body lines and gorgeous costume

colors before a background designed suggestively to heighten the pervading mood.

Max Reinhardt brought the mimo-drama to its most effective proportions in "Sumurun" and "The Miracle." In examining the sensational qualities of these two productions, one wonders whether Gordon Craig's failure to perfect the mimo-drama was due so much to lack of practical initiative as to an inherent disparity between the wordless drama form and the ideal he had in mind. For Craig is the poet at heart, instinctively shrinking from what is sensational or bizarre, and aiming to appeal quietly to the senses, and through them to some spiritual faculty which he insists is independent of the emotions and intellect, but is equally deep; whereas the mimo-drama, deprived of the appeal of subtleties of thought, that can be brought out only in dialogue, tends naturally to primitive stories worked out in violent action, with the accompaniment of brilliant color, massive grouping and impassioned dancing. Reinhardt is not at all the poet, seeking to purvey quietly sensuous and delicately spiritual adventures. He desires nothing better than to overwhelm the senses and thrill the surface emotions, and the new form came to him perfectly adapted to his talents. With his genius for organization he gathered about him a group of artists who were not hopelessly soaked in the traditions of the existing theatre, and together they evolved "Sumurun," "The Miracle," and other revolutionary productions.

"Sumurun" may be taken as a typical example of the mimo-drama. The production worked out an Arabian Nights story in pantomime, a tale heavy with the passion of the East, wherein there is the double thread of the love-story of Nur-al-Din, a young cloth-merchant, and Sumurun, the favorite wife of the old Sheik, and that of the young Sheik and the Beautiful Slave of Fatal Enchantment. The two motives are intertwined in a meshwork of love and hate, of jealousy and revenge, of lust and mur-der—but after all the story is chiefly a framework on which to build scene after scene of Oriental pag-eantry, of moving pattern of costume and setting, of passionate dancing.

"Sumurun" is typical of the æsthetic drama in three ways: first, in the totality of conception, the fidelity to a single mood of exotic richness; the play is not conceived in one mood, the setting in another, the lighting in another; line and mass blend with color, color with lighting, lighting with music, and music with story, the whole affording a single sensu-ous impression; second, in the emphasis upon the way in which the thing is done rather than upon what is done: there is little interest in the moral and little in the story-growth, but a continuous enchantment of the senses by decorative beauty of movement, danc-ing, and background pattern; it is clearly a visually

effective rather than a psychologically moving drama;
and third, in the setting: for here are simple, neutrally-toned backgrounds, that never distract the eye
from the figures on the stage, that suggest the pervading mood subtly, creating an Oriental atmosphere with the slightest of means: sometimes with
mere hanging curtains, and again with a flat wall,
neutral in tone, against which the gorgeously costumed actors stand out in flaming contrast.

Professor Reinhardt's other notable mimo-drama,
"The Miracle," based upon the legend which Maeterlinck treated poetically in his "Sister Beatrice,"
was less violent and less sensual than "Sumurun," but
in spots no less sensational.  It was no less typical
æsthetic drama, with its purely visual appeal and its
wide sweeps of pageantry.  But when one turns to
Reinhardt's other work, to such notable productions
as the "Œdipus Rex" and the Shakespearean plays,
one leaves the mimo-drama and steps almost entirely
from the field of the æsthetic play.  For these are
works that generally are classed as intellectual or
emotional drama—and yet the producer has so
changed them that the literary or story element is
almost if not entirely subordinated to the visually
decorative elements.  He cuts the dialogue, rear-
ranges the scenes, and otherwise distorts the original,
until he has the material in the form that is theatrically most effective.  The result is psychologic drama
staged æsthetically.  The process really amounts to

the "re-theatralizing" of plays that had been considered as chiefly literary, and therefore had been staged with entire negligence of the more theatric elements. Gordon Craig makes a clear distinction between his work that is typically theatric, consisting of the creation of marionette productions and mimo-dramas, and his interpretative work in staging literary plays, considering the latter merely the fitting of another art into a setting in the theatre and refraining from change. But Reinhardt brings every creative faculty to bear on the chosen play, ruthlessly cutting, shifting, adding. The method is a worthy one, if the director is an artist; and certain of the Reinhardt productions have brought a new breath of life to the shelf-plays so treated. And elsewhere, in more sensitive hands, new beauties have been brought into productions that before had been only partially effective without the full visual appeal. Thus the Moscow Art Theatre's production of "The Blue Bird" afforded a pleasure that was only half realized from the English and American productions —even though the latter were above the average in their respective countries. The Russians saturated the several settings with the symbolism that underlies the play, thus making fuller and richer its poetic charm, and they added decorative outer appeal. This way of theatralizing the drama, of enriching the playwright's work by passing the production through the mind of a creative artist-director, who conceives every detail of setting and staging in the true spirit of the original, is being put into practice in Moscow by Constantin Stanislavsky, in Paris by Jacques Rouché, in Budapest by Alexander Hevesi, and in a dozen German theatres by such men as Georg Fuchs, Ottomar Starke, and Professor Reinhardt. It is a phase of progress in the theatre that is less a distinct new form of æsthetic drama than a pervading influence throughout every department of activity of the theatre. The movement marks the carrying out to all other dramatic forms of the underlying principles of unity, concentration, and suggestion that are so characteristic of the æsthetic theatre.

Before leaving Reinhardt and the mimo-drama, to turn to the third definite development of the æsthetic drama, let us see what is the total importance of Reinhardt's service to the theatre. In the first place he brought the mimo-drama to proportions commercially valuable, and by so doing gave theatregoers of many countries the opportunity to see at least one form of the new æsthetic drama actually produced. Moreover he gave greater impetus than any other one man to the movement that Craig had started away from the old inartistic naturalism in setting and toward suggestive and decorative staging. He is a man of prodigious energy, with a genius for organization, and the range of his productions has been remarkably wide. But he has worked too

## THE ADORATION OF THE SHEPHERDS

*This is a scene from a Christmas play produced by the Lessing Society of Hamburg, under the direction of Emanuel Stockhausen. The simple hangings create the atmosphere of a starry night more successfully than could the most labored efforts of the naturalistic stage designer, with his real twinkling stars, and painted sky, and rising moons. The picture also illustrates the way in which masses of light and shade are made to contribute to the decorative effect.*

*(By courtesy of Emanuel Stockhausen.)*

fast to be the deep thinker and original creator that Craig is. Indeed, neither of these two men is to be considered the perfect artist of the æsthetic theatre. What certain of Craig's over-loyal friends cannot see is that in these pioneer days of the new art we need both men, the one complementing the other— the bold thinker and the bold practitioner. Reinhardt is not Craig's ideal artist of the theatre, because the director's is not the creative hand throughout; his scenario or play is by one hand, the music by another, the settings and costumes by another, and the final staging by still another; so Reinhardt is more the orchestra leader who attempts to draw out from his helpers what a master intended, than the monumental sculptor who makes his own model and then works personally with his helpers in chiselling out the final form. Moreover he has that tendency toward sensationalism which has buried the spiritual qualities of his art under a pursuit of physical excitement. Nevertheless he is one of the two great figures of the first decade of the æsthetic theatre's history; and he as much as Craig has paved the way for those artists of the future who doubtless will have the virtues of both and the faults of neither.

The third notable form of æsthetic drama, the Russian Ballet, recently blazed its way across the dramatic horizon in a path of glory that temporarily dimmed every other form. The new dance-drama, that so far exists almost entirely in the achievement of the Russians, is less true an art of the theatre than the marionette drama or the mimo-drama, since it combines dancing, which often is considered an art in itself, and music, with the more typical theatric elements. It is the art of the perfect combination of color and line and movement and music in one harmonious appeal to eye and ear.

There are three easily distinguishable sources of this sort of æsthetic drama. In the first place there is the old-time ballet, a form of dancing which was carefully nurtured under royal protection in Russia while it was dying a slow death throughout the rest of the world. Second, there was the revival of classic and æsthetic dancing that spread over Europe and America, and brought a new significance to the phrase "poetry of motion." And third, there came the Craig impulse to decorative staging. Gathering up the three elements and interweaving them with mutual enrichment, a group of Russian artists evolved the alluring dance-drama of to-day.

A story—does anyone ever remember what it was about after it is gone?—is unfolded in pantomime and dance, with a continuous moving pattern of shifting figures and group or solo dancing, before settings that are not, indeed, unobtrusive, but that take up the mood of the production and fling it back from every line and color; and through it all is the insinuating accompaniment of sympathetic music. Here is no art of dancing merely set in the theatre, with passable background, and a bit of music to tickle the ear. Rather do human figures and colors and lines and musical notes dance together in a dreamy ecstasy of harmony and rhythm, lulling our minds to sleep and intoxicating our senses. Colorful music and singing color set the mood for sensuous dances. And who can say that it is more the dancing of the ethereal Pavlowa, or the settings and costumes of a Bakst, or the music, that most certainly takes us out of earthly things? It is indeed the perfect combination of movement and decoration and music, the synthesis of all sensuous appeals, that so completely masters the audience.

This difference is notable between the Russian ballet and those other forms of æsthetic drama which Gordon Craig and Max Reinhardt have devoloped: that whereas they conceive the production as a fluctuating pattern against a neutral background, the Russians count the setting quite as compelling material as the movement in gaining artistic effect. "It is the day of the painter in the theatre," exclaims Leon Bakst exultantly. And he proceeds to design his gorgeous settings "like paintings into which the figures have not yet been painted"; and then to marshal masses of gorgeously robed figures in those settings with all the cunning of the master of decorative composition. It is the painter who sets the mood of the production as much as the writer of the scenario;

and the setting amplifies the appeal of every movement of the dancers.  In commenting upon the positive dramatic value of the setting, M. Péladan, a
French critic, notes that in the production of "Sche-
herazade," a tale of illicit love and lust and cruel
revenge in an Oriental harem, there was nowhere a
bit of white in the decoration or costumes; for white
is the color of innocence, and here there was room
only for the greens, the blues, the oranges, the reds,
the sensuous colors that furthered the sensual appeal; that built up a flaming riot of color to bear
in upon the senses with an insinuating pleading parallel to that of the dancing and music.

If Gordon Craig is the poet of the æsthetic theatre, striving to enchant the senses and the imagination, and Max Reinhardt the theatre showman, aiming to overwhelm the senses and thrill the surface
emotions, Leon Bakst is the Orientalist ravishing the
eye with a primitive pagan appeal.  He is the greatest of the artist-designers of the Russian ballet;
his sketches for costumes and settings mark him as
one of the finest colorists of contemporary graphic
art, and the dance-dramas he has staged earn him a
place above his fellows of the theatre.  And yet
there are others of these Russians who are doing big
things for the æsthetic theatre; among the designers,
Benois, Roerich, Anisfeld, and Golovine; and the
directors, Diaghelew and Fokine.

To say, as have many impetuous critics, that here

at last is *the* great art of the theatre, that the Russian Ballet will dominate the theatre of the future, is nonsense. The dance-drama is gorgeous entertainment, and it affords an artistic experience that is sweet and new. But when we have recovered from the first intoxication of it we shall see that there are soberer and deeper phases of drama that are not so easily to be brushed from their places in the affections of mankind; we shall continue to enjoy the old and more nourishing fare, and when the chance comes to indulge in this, the champagne of the theatre, as it were, we shall welcome the rare treat joyously but moderately.

And that is in some measure the attitude in which we should accept all the forms of æsthetic drama that have been described: not alone the Russian Ballet, but the mimo-dramas and marionette plays. While preserving our allegiance to the dramas of emotion and thought which certainly are as vital expressions of dramatic art as any of the new forms, we yet may welcome the creations of Craig and Reinhardt and Bakst as bringing a new and very refreshing sort of beauty into the playhouse. We must recognize, too, that they have revitalized the older sorts of drama, and have brought out in them unsuspected decorative qualities. They have made over the art of drama until it again is fit to appear in the theatre; and they have splendidly widened its scope.

III

THE NEW ENGLISH DRAMATISTS

# THE NEW ENGLISH DRAMATISTS

Of the several dramatic "schools" of modern times the English to-day is emerging as the most vital and most lastingly significant. Of the other movements, that Northern one which flowered so beautifully, and yet in some ways so forbiddingly, in the art of Ibsen, Strindberg, and Björnson, alone equals the English in importance. There was a time when the achievement of Hauptmann and Sudermann, and the promise of Wedekind and the younger Germans, seemed to foreshadow a great modern dramatic school in Germany; but now the pioneers seem to be written out, and the Viennese Schnitzler alone from the German-speaking countries is internationally important. But in spite of all his grace and charming lightness of touch, his insidious cynicisms and refinements of sensuality mark him as the last flickering rather than the first fire of a new development. And certainly in France, where the three really notable dramatists are so widely separated in ideals and in methods as Maeterlinck, Rostand and Brieux, there is nothing approaching a school. Mae-

terlinck is a law unto himself, and Rostand is hardly
less independent of his contemporaries; and certainly
Brieux has more in common with Shaw and Galsworthy than with any living Frenchman.

The England that gave birth to Gordon Craig,
the pioneer of the æsthetic theatre movement, and
then cast out that genius and closed its theatres to the
æsthetic drama, opened its arms wide to that other
new form, the drama of thought, that had its birth
and came to its first perfection in foreign lands; so
that to-day, while the æsthetic theatre is typically
a Continental art, the new intensive drama is flowering in England more beautifully than in any other
country.  Indeed, in the theatre of thought, the English school, as a group, is by every test the greatest
in achievement and the greatest in promise in the
world to-day.  Though it is only in the imperfect
beginnings of its development—though it seems to
foreshadow greater glories to come—it already
forces recognition not only as the most significant
English flowering since Elizabethan days, but as one
of the two very great developments in modern dramatic history.

The fact that three dramatists of the brilliancy
and solid worth of Bernard Shaw, John Galsworthy
and J. M. Barrie are writing contemporaneously
would make the time a notable one dramatically.
And when one adds to their achievement that of J.
M. Synge and St. John Hankin, whose work is ended,

and remembers that John Masefield, Granville Barker and Arnold Bennett still are working toward the
same ideals, the day seems rich indeed. And very
recently a newer and younger group have started
the impetus anew: Stanley Houghton, and Elizabeth
Baker, and Githa Sowerby. As many more might be
named as probable important dramatists of to-morrow.

It might be objected that the grouping of such
diversely great men as Shaw, Barrie and Galsworthy
precludes the use of the term "School." Shaw with
his brilliancy of dialogue and his startling originality,
Barrie with his undercurrent of fantasy, Galsworthy
with his somber power, are indeed different. Nevertheless there is a pervading current through all their
work that marks them distinctly as of one time and
one movement: a straightforward method of play-
building, a haunting social note, a peculiarly modern
attitude of mind.

If one desired to chart the growth of the modern
drama of thought, it would be necessary to go back
to the French dramatists who first began to modify
the artificial standards of the Scribe-Sardou School:
to Augier and Dumas the younger; then to turn to
Ibsen, the great revolutionist; and then to draw a
number of parallel lines for the concurrent developments in Germany, Russia, Scandinavia, and England—with a single thread to France, and hardly
half a thread to Italy, Spain, and the United States.

But while it is easy to trace the influence of Ibsen upon all the later dramatists, and to recognize the interweaving nature of the later developments, it is easy also to underestimate the creative element in each group, the influence of national life and ideals, and the playwrights' innate originality. Thus the current English development, while clearly owing an immense debt to Ibsen, and while clearly allied to the movement that produced Hauptmann and Wedekind, is yet in some measure an original growth: neither a mere sudden after-flaring of the torch of Ibsenism, nor a mere relighting of the dead fire of the German or the Scandinavian schools. In a very true sense, the new English drama is the result of an independent attempt to be at once true to the times, true to human nature, and true to art.

The real extent of the English dramatists' debt to Ibsen never can be measured. Doubtless the straightforward art of the Norwegian master started the revolution against the old insincere and artificial forms in England as elsewhere. And every contemporary playwright follows Ibsen's technique more closely than that of any earlier master, because Ibsen most perfectly fitted his dramas to the limitations of the modern playhouse, and because he moulded his material into the form best suited to stir modern audiences. The new artists of the theatre have taken his compactness of form and his sincerity of treatment; but the fine thing about them is that they accept him open-mindedly, without following him blindly. They recognize that he is not of their country, or their time (for the world has taken mighty strides forward since he ceased to write); and being true to themselves, they follow him only in so far as his art is universally appealing. They have turned in the same way, though with less to learn, to Shakespeare and the Greeks; and they may quite as readily find bits of inspiration in Strindberg or Brieux.

Since the drama of thought does not, like the æsthetic drama, imply a complete reversal of the principles of the old emotional drama, but rather has picked up the drama of emotion, perfected it, and augmented its effectiveness by adding a deeper and more significant sort of appeal, it is clear that the growth of the one form in England has not been independent of the growth of the other. One might name the Pinero of "The Second Mrs. Tanqueray" as a direct forerunner of the new race of dramatists. This play marks the point at which the typical practitioner of the drama of emotion approaches closest to the drama of thought, to the intensive idea-play. But when one places the Pinero production beside one of the socially effective plays of Galsworthy, the wide gap between the best of the emotional plays and the typical theme-play is only too evident. Not only is the deeper social significance of the latter very clearly shadowed forth, but one is very unpleasantly impressed with the older dramatist's dependence upon the trickery of the Sardou well-made-play: the type characterization, the stock situations, and the lack of adequate motivation. Even "The Second Mrs. Tanqueray" exhibits momentary lapses to a patent theatricality, and one recognizes in it immediately the inevitable figure of the family confidant, and touches of the old "comic relief."

It is not to be inferred that the drama whose only reason for being is in its power to stir the emotions has no legitimate place in the theatre. The drama of emotion provides keen and wholesome enjoyment and affords actual new emotional experience to the theatregoer; moreover it has a sort of social value, since it builds sympathy. But it never can be as vital art as the drama that combines emotional and intellectual appeal, that stirs men's souls and leaves the after-impulse to do. Arthur Pinero and Henry Arthur Jones in a way foreran the new movement: they developed the drama of emotion from its degraded melodrama form to the best of which it is capable; and it is doubtful whether the drama of thought could have flourished in the English theatre, had they not made that advance. But Pinero and Jones left off just where Galsworthy and Shaw and Barker began; they never for a moment stepped over into the field of the drama of sincerity, into the field of the social play. St. John Hankin did see the new ideal, and even though he did not have the originality of a Shaw, or the power of a Galsworthy, he wrote plays which naturally take place within the new movement.   Even Oscar Wilde was closer to the new school than Pinero and Jones, for he doubtless had visions of more vital things than he accomplished; but he fell prey to his own brilliant facility, and to the prevailing notion that anything that entertained was good dramatic art.

Let us see in just what ways the new English drama differs from the old, and incidentally how it differs from the similar developments in other countries.

It is not possible to pick any one play and say that the single example exhibits perfectly all the distinguishing qualities of any school.   But from the whole body of work one may discover the common ideal toward which the several playwrights are working, each to the extent of his ability, and each in his own way.   What is it that the new English dramatists are trying to do?   What ideal emerges from the multiple efforts of the artists of this latest school?

The distinguishing quality of the new drama is *sincerity,* in theme, in treatment of story, and in technical construction.   Mainly it is a reaction from the false theatricality and shallow sentimentality of the play of twenty years ago.   The refreshing breath of sincerity stirs through its every part.   The pas-

sion for truth is, indeed, so marked that the English
group has been termed "The School of Sincerity."

The new drama usually is close to contemporary
life in theme. It has not an empty shell of dramatic
story, like the farces and melodramas of other days,
that left the mind a blank. Nor is its core of
thought based upon the false premises and cynical
attitude of the French triangle plays. The new
drama treats themes that are deeply human and
vitally stirring. The outward personal plot is il-
lumined by an inward *social* plot. Because the play
reflects current thought, the surface character-story
is shot through with underlying humanitarian motive. The story is developed as typical of deep social truth. As Ibsen was concerned with the faint
beginnings of the feminist movement, the newer
dramatists are concerned with its fully developed
and swiftly flowing current; as Hauptmann found
dramatic possibilities in industrial life twenty years
ago, his English followers sift to the bottom the
more acute industrial crises of to-day. Sociology,
religion, science, yield up their themes to the theatre,
to be thrown back at mankind in an emotional form
more compelling than argument or preaching or
teaching. And yet in the best plays the theme never
obtrudes itself apart from character; it is expressed
in terms of emotionally affecting story. The drama
is brought close to the problems of life without

THE NEW ENGLISH DRAMATISTS 75

breaking down the backgrounds of humanity and beauty and mystery that characterize all art.

In the treatment of the plot-materials, in the fashioning of the story, the passion for sincerity is most marked. The new dramatists use no tricks of appeal. All those old melodramatic devices that so easily trick the audience into purely momentary tears or laughter, leaving only a sense of emptiness, are foreign to their work. All the old false type characters are scorned. The development of those forces that are psychologically subtle is recognized as action of a more dramatic sort than physical violence. The inevitable changes of character and of society are recognized as material more appealing than chance happenings. Nothing is introduced because it is sensational. A play of tragic atmosphere throughout is not brought to an improbable happy close, just to give the public what it wants. The drama is completed logically, without straining to add that theatric touch of finality which will allow the spectator to go home without any further thought for the characters or matter of the play. There is no overlaid comic relief; and there are no inorganic incidents that are interesting in themselves, but extraneous to the dramatic design.

In the building of their dramatic structure the new artists seek first for unity. In their technique there is a new firmness of structure, a new feeling for sequential growth. Even their "exposition,"

to use a technical term, is so woven into the rising
action that it is an integral part of the play rather
than a mere introduction. Without copying the
tricks of the old dramatic schools, they have recognized that there is a certain crescendo form of action that evokes the greatest emotional response
from the audience. They develop this crescendo of
action with a new economy of means, and a new
feeling for adequate motivation. The compactness,
swiftness, and tenseness of their action have read a
new meaning into the word "dramatic."

With all their sincerity of treatment, with their
seriousness of theme, with their scorning of theatricality and sensationalism in story, and with their
new integrity of structure, they bring that other
quality of great drama : imaginative beauty. In their
best work there is literary distinction, the poetic
touch. Their best plays light up even the unpleasant
with that inner beauty which is the final test of all
art.

There have been attempts to label the new group
of dramatists as realists, or idealists, or romanticists, or of what-not school. But they are elusive
prey for the artistic cataloguers. It happens that
if a man writes a play of unmistakable genius, there
is always a commentator to call him realistic because his work is so human, and another to call him
idealistic because he is so finely eclectic in his choice
of material, and because he lights up that material

with an inner ennobling beauty. The trouble lies
in that there are no standard definitions of realism
and idealism and romanticism. If they are contrasting terms, so that a dramatist who may be labelled with one, cannot partake of the qualities of
the others, then the new artists belong to no one
of these groups. They are realistic to the extent
of reflecting current life; but they strike to the
deeper springs of human action, instead of merely
touching the surface aspects; their aim is not the
sort of realism that photographically delineates a
sordid segment of life. They are impressionistic
in that they are true to their own impressions, rather
than painting exactly what they see with their physical eyes. They are idealistic with an idealism that
has its roots in the truths of life and the mysteries
of the soul; not at all with the insincere, unreal
and unconvincing idealism of the old artificial theatre. If romance means something entirely removed
from the times and places we know, they are not
romanticists; but they are the truest sort of romanticists if romance is merely that permanently appealing sense of spiritual adventure which underlies
the material aspects of life, that intangible something to which the passion of the poet responds.
Perhaps it is because they are so true to themselves
and so careless of established dramatic boundaries,
that they so surely defy classification. They do not
set out with the definite purpose of being realists,

or idealists, or romanticists; the result is that they are merely sincere—more sincere than any other group of dramatists for many centuries.

John Galsworthy is at once the most typical dramatist of the new movement and (since Shaw seems to be travelling backward) the most promising. He most perfectly interweaves, at least in his best plays, the story and the theme, the emotion plot and the thought plot. His is most typically the "social" drama. While his characterization so preserves the individual note that our sympathies are held throughout the action, at the end we always are conscious that the figures are social types. The audience is left with a new insight into, and with a new impulse to think about, some humanly significant problem.

Galsworthy is the one man to whom the world may look most hopefully for the further flowering of the drama of thought; for his is the double equipment of dramatic craftsman and literary artist. In his passion for literary expression he does not scorn to consider the limitations of the modern theatre; and yet in bowing to those limitations he does not violate his artistic conscience. He is the poet, the true artist, come again into the theatre. Above all he is sincere—always true to himself.

Galsworthy's personal contribution to the drama of sincerity includes seven plays. Of these "Strife" and "The Silver Box" perhaps are most characteristic. Both are plays that are alive with emotional appeal and that carry trenchant social messages. In them the dramatist preserves his impartial attitude as artist, the judicial attitude that merely brings forth the evidence, without stating the case of one side or the other: without bitterness showing forth the effects of a social system through an emotional crisis. "Justice" is the third of the vital social plays, but is less a work of art and more a social document than the others. It shows lapses to the diffuseness of the novelistic form, and the central emotional motive is not so perfectly worked out. Poor Falder and Ruth Honeywill take hold of the spectators' sympathies, but Falder is rather too pale a character for chief protagonist. The play, it is said, brought about sweeping reforms in the prison system which it so mercilessly showed forth. Like certain of Brieux's plays it is worth while because it is a vitally effective social treatise, even if it is artistically defective. If Galsworthy had not written the similar plays, "The Pigeon" and "The Eldest Son" (the latter rather more brutally ironic than was necessary), and the dissimilar "Joy" and "The Little Dream," he still would have stood in the first rank of the dramatists of thought, by reason of the three that are such powerful intensive dramas of thought.

The greatest figure of the new group is perhaps the least important as playwright. Bernard Shaw is by far the most brilliant writer of dialogue and the most daring thinker who has come into the English theatre; but he is not at all the consummate dramatist.  He is incomparable as moralist and sociological reformer; and no one has so successfully brought the theatre into the service of the social movement.  But as art his work is defective.  He does not realize that art carries a message through emotional experience, and not by preaching at or discussion before an audience; and he has not mastered play technique.  At first he swallowed whole the method of play structure of the Sardou-Pinero-Jones school—comic relief, type figures, and all—and he employed "the long arm of coincidence" in a way that would have brought the blush of shame to even Pinero and Jones in their early days.  Then, becoming impatient of all rules, he dropped the artificial "well-made-play" form, for no form at all. The more's the pity, for if Shaw had possessed Ibsen's technical excellence, and had preserved the point of view of the artist, he would have been greater as dramatist than Ibsen: for his thought is more trenchant, and his dialogue is more brilliant. But he remains the incomparable philosopher and the second rate playwright of the English theatre.

In the early group of "pleasant" plays Shaw still had the dramatic instinct, and "Candida" and "Arms and the Man" are among the most delightful actable comedies of recent times—and even the implausible "You Never Can Tell" has a certain dramatic effectiveness. In the early plays of social purpose, of the type of "Mrs. Warren's Profession," the dramatic element still is mixed with the moralistic; then as the years go by the dialectician gains on the playwright, until in "Getting Married" the moralist has completely conquered the dramatist. Even in "Man and Superman," which is in some respects one of the most delightful and most important plays of the new movement, the action is so clogged with philosophic discussion and with inorganic incident that the drama takes important place on the bookshelf rather than on the stage. Just as Shakespeare is the incomparable poet, the unrivalled literary artist, rather than the incomparable dramatist, so Shaw is the great social thinker, and even the great humorist, rather than the great dramatic artist. He really has advanced the new movement more by stirring contemporary playwrights to think deeply than by his direct contribution to the theatre.

Granville Barker is a follower of Shaw, and has much of the Shavian independence of thought—but without the Shavian incisiveness. On the other hand, Barker is by far the better technician. "The Marrying of Ann Leete," "Waste," and "The Voysey Inheritance" have a definite progression of incident and an adequate motivation that are foreign to most of the Shaw plays. The worst fault in Barker's dramas is an occasional diffuseness of dialogue, an

extension of the introductory conversations to subjects that are entirely foreign to the central theme
and story.  The opening act of "Waste" especially
is marked by irrelevancies.  In the attempt to create
atmosphere, no doubt, the dramatist has sacrificed
terseness of expression and compactness.  In the
later "Madras House" Barker unfortunately has
followed the Shaw faults as well as the Shaw virtues, and produced the least dramatic of his works.
It is to be hoped that he will develop along the lines
indicated in the earlier plays—and then he may hold
the place that he has taken rather provisionally
among the four or five leaders of the intensive
drama movement.

J. M. Barrie is more independent of his contemporaries than any other dramatist of the new group.
Perhaps half of his plays cannot by any straining
be squeezed into conformance with the definition
of the drama of thought.  But while the others have,
as a rule, touches of the Barrie fantasy and an undercurrent of sentimentalism, they are distinctly of
the idea-play type.  It is a long stride from "Peter
Pan" to "The Twelve Pound Look" and "What
Every Woman Knows," and especially to the later
plays of the type of the ironic little "Half an Hour,"
and one fancies that Barrie never would have taken
it had there not been a Shaw and a Galsworthy to
show that there was legitimate dramatic material
in the deeper phases of life.  But Barrie saw the

new light, and coming to it, brought in a romantic
note that the intensive drama so far had lacked.  If
Galsworthy lessened the gap between realism and
idealism, Barrie showed that the old conception
of realism and romanticism as opposite extremes
was false.  And he proved that the literary artist
turned dramatist can retain his literary charm while
being true to the theatre.

Because Arnold Bennett never freed himself from
the novelist's viewpoint and the novelist's methods,
as did Barrie and Galsworthy, his plays never have
been entirely effective in the theatre.  He is distinctly of the new movement, when one analyzes
what he is trying to do; but his work is defective
because he has not thrown off the novelist's diffuseness of form.  One feels, too, that he has not the
passion for sincerity that marks several of his fellow dramatists.  "The Great Adventure" is a dramatization of an earlier novel, and naturally would not
exhibit typical dramatic tension and compactness.
But even those other plays that were written primarily for the theatre indicate an incomplete understanding of the rigid economy of means necessary
to the building up of a logical play structure.  Thus
"What the Public Wants" when put on the stage had
delightful moments, as do all the Bennett productions, but somehow one felt that here was a carica-
ture of the real idea-play: that here was a half-
hearted or a blundering attempt to treat sincerely

a live social theme. It is quite conceivable that Arnold Bennett believes what he has so cleverly said and so widely published about the uselessness of studying dramatic technique. Perhaps when his hasty self-sufficiency has been cooled somewhat by his comparative failure in the theatre, he will take pains to construct dramas that are intensely dramatic as well as clever and incidentally delightful.

If Bennett must be included in the group of new dramatists because he has written plays which are faintly reflective of the new ideals, there are several "one-play" dramatists who are equally entitled to places because each has written a single drama that is very typical of the school. John Masefield's "Tragedy of Nan" is one of the finest accomplishments of the younger generation. It adds notable literary beauty to a typically dramatic idea-play. In some ways it exhibits as perfectly as any other drama the realization of the new dual realistic-idealistic aim: the modern desire for greater literal knowledge but for greater idealism in interpreting that knowledge. Stanley Houghton is another dramatist whose single important play links him unmistakably with Galsworthy and Shaw and Barker. "Hindle Wakes" is a vigorous close-knit study of English life, fearlessly unconventional in thought and presented with great technical ability.[1]   Githa Sow-

[1] The unfortunate death of Stanley Houghton, in early manhood, has occurred since this essay was written.

erby, in "Rutherford and Son," wrote a typically powerful and compact intensive drama, that was sombre but gripping.

St. John Hankin was one of the pioneers of the new English group and a number of his plays are distinctly worth while. But he lacked to some measure the depth of thought and the power of his better known followers.

The Irish School of playwrights is distinctly allied with the group that has been discussed; but the note of nationalism is so inbred that the development must be considered as in some measure a separate growth. The Irish plays, from Synge to St. John Ervine, are idea-plays, and they blend realism and idealism and symbolism as perfectly as any dramas of the new movement. But always there is a distinct difference: the universal social message is less stressed, the racial peculiarities are noticeable, and there is a poetic conception, a literary beauty, that seldom has been surpassed in any body of drama. From Yeats, in whom the poetry is more important than the dramatic element, and Synge, who brought the poetic conception to everyday life in some of the most remarkable productions of modern times, to Lady Gregory and Ervine, there is a wide range of excellence. But all, with the possible exception of Yeats, are distinctly products of the time, reflecting the worldwide new spirit.

For the rest there are half a dozen who, in

achievement or promise, are typically dramatists of
thought; but a word must suffice for each.  Elizabeth
Baker wrote "Chains," typical of the close-range
point of view and the straightforward technique of
the new school.  Cosmo Hamilton, in "The Blindness of Virtue," wrote a play with a real message,
but his treatment was less sincere than one might
wish; the sentimental touches and the comic relief
were too clearly laid on according to an artificial
and outworn method.  And Macdonald Hastings,
Israel Zangwill and Gilbert Cannan all have contributed in some degree to the movement's progress.

In conclusion it is interesting to note that the
actual advance from the traditional forms of dramatic entertainment to the infinitely more vital and
artistic new forms has come not in London,
the English centre of dramatic commerce, but in
"the provinces."  Though the "Stage Society"
first cradled the movement in London, much as
the famous " Théâtre Libre" cradled the corresponding development in Paris, the later growth
occurred away from the capital.  And just as
the most promising forces in the American theatre
to-day are at work in the scattered experimental
theatres and at the universities—indeed anywhere
but on Broadway—so the new English drama has
been developing and is being developed chiefly in
such experimental or at least non-commercial playhouses as Miss Horniman's Repertory Theatre in

Manchester, and The Abbey Theatre in Dublin. The repertory theatre movement is growing with remarkable rapidity, and the close correspondence of its development with that of the new drama indicates more than a mere coincidence. The repertory theatres not only are calling forth increasingly fine plays from the new race of dramatists, but they are breeding a new generation of actors competent to interpret the drama of thought. Miss Horniman's remarkably capable company, with the wonderful Irene Rooke, recently proved to Americans, in an engagement all too short, how much finer the new drama really is than the old, provided the interpretation is adequate. The cycle of plays included Galsworthy's "The Silver Box," Shaw's "Candida," Bennett's "What the Public Wants," and Masefield's "Tragedy of Nan." Its effectiveness proved how satisfying the new English drama is for lovers of the serious art of the theatre, for those who care for the sort of drama that stirs something deeper than surface tears and idle laughter.

# IV

## THE AMERICAN PLAYWRIGHT AND THE DRAMA OF SINCERITY

# THE AMERICAN PLAYWRIGHT AND
# THE DRAMA OF SINCERITY

Of the two deeply significant movements in the present-day theatre, only one has reached the American playhouse in any appreciable measure. In European countries the æsthetic theatre movement has grown to such vital proportions that it is absorbing the genius of some of the world's most original artists; but the American dramatist has contributed practically nothing to its development. Whether through some inherent lack of creative ability in the field of impressionistic drama, or through the outward organization of the "show business" in America, little effort has been directed to the production of purely "æsthetic" plays. Aside from certain forms of pageantry and the charming production of "The Yellow Jacket" there is little to record that is even remotely suggestive of the ideals of Gordon Craig and Max Reinhardt and Leon Bakst.

What progress has been made by the Americans as a part of the recent worldwide expansion of the activities of the theatre has been in the direction of the new intensive drama, the drama of thought. To perfect the old drama of emotion and to add a new significance to it—as the new English dramatists are doing—rather than to strike into the untried field of decorative or æsthetic drama, clearly is the aim of the younger (and the only important) generation of American playwrights.

"The drama of sincerity" is the most recent and the most vital development of the psychologic drama. It is the latest flowering of the drama of combined emotional and intellectual appeal, which first blossomed in the work of Ibsen. It is the art of the English "school of sincerity" in playwriting: the art of John Galsworthy and Bernard Shaw, for instance, and of J. M. Barrie, and Granville Barker and Stanley Houghton.

The quality that chiefly distinguishes this group of English dramatists is *sincerity*. They strive above all to be true to themselves. But as they are men who live deeply and study and write passionately, they are at the same time true to life and to art. Their plays are truly dramatic, rather than theatric; they are natural, but not slavishly photographic: they incorporate only detail that is organic to the dramatic design; they interpret rather than imitate; they deal with inner spiritual forces, rather than with outward melodramatic happenings; they affect the emotions, and indirectly the mind, by a quiet development of character, rather than pleasing the

outward senses and surface feelings by sensationalism. Their work usually is *social* drama in the
best sense. It is humanitarian, because they reflect
contemporary life, and the spirit of the age is humanitarian.

These men are stripping the theatre production
of all sensational incident, of all those details that
are interesting but unimportant, and of all the old
insincere adjuncts of plot, acting and setting; taking the remaining essential skeleton of unified story,
they are clothing it with imaginative beauty, making
it emotionally appealing, and adding to it a social
significance. In their best work they are not losing
the sense of the sweetness of life in a sense of the
finality of evil. They end their plays seriously and
in the same pervading mood as they began them,
without straining to close with either an improbable
happiness or an unlikely death. From beginning to
end they are sincere.

It is this sort of drama that the American playwright has in mind—that is, if he is concerned with
the theatre as an art rather than as a business; in
short, if he is sincere. If he is passionately fond
of his art, and alive to every development of that
art and to its relation to life, he cannot but see
that the impending vital development of American
drama will be toward the ideals that Galsworthy
and his fellow dramatists are realizing in England.

That the influence of the new English dramatists

already has been felt in America, one who has
studied the productions of the past two or three
seasons cannot doubt. Already there are welcome
signs that the American writer for the theatre is
striving to produce a body of drama close to the
people, reflecting the life of the times, touched with
imaginative beauty, and emotionally appealing in a
sincere way. Indeed the signs are so evident that
it is worth while to enquire wherein and why he has
failed as compared with his English brother.

In the first place it may be remarked that the
trouble lies neither in the material nor in the demand,
but in the playwright. The material is at hand and
the public is ready; the failure lies with the artist.
A condition precedent to any great development of
art is a period of wide social, industrial and political activity. By that token surely in America to-
day the time is ripe for a flowering of art. Certainly at no time or place in the world's history has
life been lived more widely, more deeply, more intensely. Not only does the average man have a
wider range of physical experience than ever before;
but the artist-dreamer, the man who sees down to
the underlying causes of material things, enjoys a
wider range of spiritual adventure than ever before.
In the pulsating life of the American people, from
the crowded cities to the broad solitary spaces of
the plains and mountains, there are themes and stories for innumerable gripping dramas. It is not

the material that is lacking, but the dramatist who can realize and convey the beauty that underlies the virility of American life.

It is sometimes objected, generally by the theatre "manager," that the public is not ready to accept the drama of sincerity, that there is no audience for "serious" work; or again that it will not accept plays by American dramatists with American characters and ideas, except in the more sensational and more obvious types. The objection might have been valid ten, or even five, years ago. But to-day it is not. The popular success of the plays of Barrie; the increasing response to the offerings of Galsworthy, Masefield, Synge, Bennett, and Shaw, when adequately acted; the success of Mrs. Fiske, Mary Shaw and Alla Nazimova in Ibsen's dramas; the sustained support of Winthrop Ames' series of "advanced" plays, and of the offerings of the Chicago Fine Arts Theatre; and the growing interest in the repertory of the Irish Players—these and many more indications point to the existence of an ever-increasing large audience for the drama of sincerity. And if the play has the universal element in it, the American audience will accept it whether it treats of American life, or English, or Norwegian, or of any other.

It has been suggested that the trouble with the theatre in France is that French audiences are oversophisticated: that the French dramatist no longer can touch the jaded sensibilities of the theatregoer except by strained situation and violent emotion. American audiences are emphatically not in that position; they are not over-sophisticated, and they are becoming increasingly cultivated and eager for dramas that appeal subtly to the emotions and intellect. They rightly demand plays that entertain —no drama or picture or poem is worthy of the name of art if it does not hold the interest—but they no longer demand insincerity. The American playwright who, instead of melodramatizing the outward aspects of American life, dramatizes its inner spiritual motives and its subtler underlying forces, will find an immense audience ready and eager for him. The material is at hand and the audience is ready; the American theatre only awaits the dramatic poet-craftsman.

The much-discussed failure of the American playwright is only a comparative failure. Judged by comparison with a Galsworthy or a Barrie, his achievement certainly is a failure. But the present writer, and every fair commentator, must recognize that the present stage of the art in this country is an indication of a very true progress when contrasted with conditions of ten years ago. The advance during the past decade has been very real and very encouraging. And the writer believes in the assured coming of a great body of vital American drama quite as confidently as he does in the future of American painting or American sculpture. But granting the real progress of the past and the bright promise of the future, it is none the less true that the American dramatist of to-day *is* a failure if judged by his contemporaries on the other side of the Atlantic.

In answering *wherein* American plays fail, one may sum up the indictment in three counts: first, that they have too much untempered strength, and not enough depth and subtlety; second, that they lack the poetic touch, the sense of beauty; and third that they too often are marred by the attempt to give the public what it wants, chiefly in comic relief and in melodramatic turns.

American plays suffer from a surfeit of strength, of force. There is a Broadway term which exactly expresses the apotheosis of this quality: "the play with a punch." The term carries its own condemnation. The play with a punch exists for the punch, and not for the dramatic building up of a story from subtle beginnings to an emotional climax; it is just what it connotes: the prizefight element in drama— brute force and shock. It is a dramatization of the violent moments of life. It deals with surface aspects rather than underlying causes. Great drama always is strong and direct and forceful; but its strength always is blended with subtlety. American drama has the strength, but seldom the tempering subtlety. It is admirably direct, but it is shallow.

The poetic element is lacking in the productions

of American playwrights.   When their plays are
worth while for poetic quality, as Percy Mackaye's
"Sappho and Phaon," or Josephine Preston Peabody's "The Piper," they take rank as literature
rather than as drama.   In the actable plays of the
day there is not the poetic touch, the inner illuminating beauty that would make them great art.   In the
dramas of Galsworthy and Barrie there is a poetic
element, a literary distinction, a pervading beauty
that cannot be defined, and yet is always sensed by
the reader or spectator.   It is the touch of the
poet, the artist, the dreamer, that has distinguished
all great drama from Æschylus to Ibsen; it is the
quality that makes plays eternally lasting and universally appealing.   That quality is seldom felt in
American plays.

The American playwrights as a group have been
severely criticized by foreign commentators for pandering so largely to public taste.   It is only too true
that the majority of them have sacrificed their independence of viewpoint and their ideals of art, to give
the public what it wants—or rather what the manager supposes it wants.   In one sense art exists vitally
only in its resultant effect upon an audience.   There
is no more futile abortion in the whole field of art
than a true drama that never is acted before an audience.   So the dramatist to a certain extent must
shape his plays to the demands of the audiences
of the time.   But that is not a valid excuse for de-

basing the drama for the ever-present vulgar portion of the public.  The fine thing about the situation in the dramatic world to-day is that there is a very large cultivated, serious-minded audience that is ready to accept sincere drama.  One can call to mind half a dozen recent American plays that would have been just as effective and just as appealing, had they been stripped of their comic relief, their superfluous sensationalism, and their insincere endings— provided, of course, the dramatist making the changes had been possessed of true dramatic power, had been a true artist of the theatre.  There is nothing inherently repelling about sincerity in a drama.  But it is much easier to write a play that will entertain with comic relief, and melodramatic situation, and insincere sentimentality, than to fashion a drama at once sincere and grippingly interesting.  The American playwrights, with very few exceptions, have failed to show themselves capable of producing drama that is true enough to art to be able to draw audiences without the aid of added insincere and inorganic attractions.

Having recognized some of the qualities wherein they have failed, one may well ask *why* they have failed.  The causes are many, but it is worth while to trace one or two of the principal ones.

The lack of subtlety and lack of depth are due in some measure to the fact that our playwrights have been recruited largely from the ranks of newspaper writers.  To mention only a few who come to mind immediately:  Eugene Walter, Augustus Thomas, George Ade, William C. DeMille, and A. E. Thomas.  The newspaper men have brought to the theatre an admirable directness and a "dramatic sense."  But necessarily they have been trained to see rapidly the surface aspects of life, rather than to ponder deeply on the underlying motives and causes.  They have the reportorial instinct for outward sensational situations, but not the dramatist's insight into motivation and character growth.  They display a wonderful facility in grasping vital stories and setting them forth in quick forceful strokes; but they too seldom free themselves from journalistic haste and shallowness.

Another large group of writers for the theatre —and especially of the older men—have been brought up within the playhouse, and find it difficult to get away from what is inherently theatrical.  They have witnessed so many times the effectiveness of the old stock situations that they mistake them for the dramatic elements of life.  Men like David Belasco, who were schooled in the theatre of the eighties and nineties, cannot bring themselves to part with the melodramatic poses, the comic relief figures, and the distracting naturalisms of setting, that were so large a part of the stock in trade of the past generation of playwrights.  One cannot but feel that they often see the right goal, that they catch glimpses of the ideals of the new movement, but that theatricality and artistic insincerity are so deeply bred in them that they never can contribute vitally to American drama.

A very potent cause for the failure of the American dramatist is that he generally is too close to the glittering lights and glittering dollars of Broadway. There is in his hurried life a constant temptation to commercialize his talents. Again and again men of solid promise have lowered their ideals to produce plays that were melodramatic, or farcical, or sentimentally sweet enough to catch the "popular" taste; and others have turned their hands to the fashioning of musical comedy librettos, to satisfy the jaded appetites of the tired business man. It happens that artistic ideals once compromised are difficult to regain. Men who once have set the dollar standard above the art standard seldom return to significant creative work. There is something pathetic, as well as something fine, in the spectacle of Charles Klein—perhaps the most successful of American playwrights, according to Broadway standards—breaking all his ties in America, and sailing for England and quietude. He was big enough to see that he had lost his artistic perspective in the environment of commercialism into which he had drifted in New York. Many another writer might with advantage to his art get away from the atmosphere of the "show business" which pervades

Broadway. There is no intent to suggest that the
dramatist should isolate himself away from New
York and the other big cities. On the contrary the
great American dramatists will be distinctly of the
city. But they will know the bigness and the solitude
of the country as well. When they come to New
York's truly remarkable dramatic centre, with its
eddying life and its immense risks and gains in theatrical ventures, and its temptations to lower standards and imitate and make "successes," they will
keep their heads and see that there are more significant achievements for the man of independent
thought and high ideals. They will live the life
of the city intensely; but they will remember that
dreaming and pondering are part of the battle.
They will accept Broadway at its true value and no
more.

A more fundamental reason for the failure of
the American playwright is that in the American
theatres the play has not been the thing. The drama
has been of secondary importance to the acting and
the setting; the work of the playwright secondary
to that of manager, producer and actor. Fortunately the condition is passing, but without doubt it
has had a retarding effect upon the growth of a vital
American drama. It was not so very long ago that
the name of the playwright was as often as not
omitted from the program; and even now it is not
unusual to see the manager's and actors' names much

more conspicuously displayed than the author's. Inevitably such lack of consideration tends to degrade
the position of the playwright to that of a tradesman
rather than an artist. The "star system" has made
it appear that the work of the actor was more vital
as art than the work of the dramatist; and many a
play has been marred by being strained to fit a certain "star." We are at last learning that it is the
playwright's art which is truly creative, and that
the actor's work should be interpretative. The
dramatist should be recognized as the artist, the
actor as the tool for the accomplishment of that
artist's purpose. The average American play has
been buried, too, under all sorts of "scenic effects"
and superadded vaudeville "stunts." The manager
has counted as so much clear gain any trick of setting
or any added incident that would bring a laugh or a
round of applause from the audience, without regard
to relevance or organic connection with the essential
plot. The practice has tended to degrade the production to vaudeville standards, and to discourage
the writing of plays of unified structure, designed to
evoke a single sustained mood. Both the star system
and the managers' craze for "stage effects" have contributed substantially to the failure of the American
playwright.

It is worth while to turn for a moment to the
consideration of individual playwrights: to measure
individually the achievement and the promise of the

men who are writing to-day for the American stage.

One is likely to turn more hopefully to a man of marked poetic ability, like Percy Mackaye, than to some others who have shown more strength and dramatic directness but less literary distinction. For the poetic touch and the imaginative element are more difficult to cultivate than forcefulness and dramatic technique. Percy Mackaye began his career as dramatist with a series of plays which are more significant as literature than as drama. The most important of these, "Sappho and Phaon," has admirable flashes of true poetry, but its beauty is too reflective, and the development of its action is not quite swift and direct enough to make it emotionally appealing on the stage. "The Scarecrow" is a finer piece of work, both from the stage viewpoint and as a contribution to American literature. It strikes a note of fancy, of fantastic beauty, that is one of the saddest needs of American drama. More recently Mackaye has turned to contemporary life for his stories, recognizing perhaps that he had been working too far from the life of the people. In "Mater" and "Anti-Matrimony" he attempted to treat the social and political life in which we all are interested, in a vein of subtly bantering comedy. In "To-morrow" he tried to dramatize a great social problem. No one of the three plays has been eminently successful in the theatre; but all combine the insight of the poet and a story of the life of the day.

One feels that the fault that keeps them from being great American plays is rather one of form, of technique, than of material or of imperfect imaginative conception. It is pleasing to think that perhaps these plays mark the dramatist's transition period between his early "literary" work and a coming group of dramas that will combine his newly acquired conception of the significance of contemporary life with his early evidenced poetic qualities. American drama needs his fancy, his wit, his tenderness, and his wide reach of imagination and depth of insight. But he must gain a little more strength, a feeling for the forceful intensity of American life; and he must mould his stories in a form more compact, and one emotionally appealing and dramatically persuasive. Then it is not improbable that he will take rank as the foremost American playwright. At present he has in very generous measure those subtler qualities that his contemporaries almost totally lack; but he lacks to a certain extent the force, the dramatic directness, which is the only claim to recognition that some of the others possess.

It is hardly necessary to touch upon the work of Josephine Preston Peabody (now Mrs. Marks). She has been so successful in her chosen field of poetry that it would be unkind to judge even "The Piper" by the standards of actable drama instead of those of literature. Her plays, like the early plays of Mackaye, are dramatic poetry rather than poetic drama. But whereas Mackaye has latterly turned almost entirely to drama, and has achieved fame chiefly as a playwright, Mrs. Marks remains always first and foremost the poet. Her plays will live, but even on the stage their interest will always have a literary or historical flavor, rather than dramatic emotional appeal. In subject-matter, in the author's emphasis on material, in method of treatment, they have little in common with the work of the men whose ideals have been set up here as a standard: Galsworthy, Barrie, Shaw, and the others. Nor would any of us desire to have her strain her art to come within the limitations of the playhouse as these writers have had to do; we prefer her as the poet.

What a contrast to Mackaye is Eugene Walter! If only one could have the poetic conception and tenderness of the one combined with the sheer power and strength of the other! Walter is without a shadow of doubt the most forceful of American playwrights. But if Mackaye is too much the poet and dreamer, and too far removed from the life of the people, one feels that Walter, on the other hand, is almost too close to life, and certainly not sufficiently the thinker and the literary artist. His early play "Paid in Full," despite its great popular success, cannot be considered vital work, nor is it representative of the author. But in "The Easiest Way" and "Fine Feathers" Walter is at his best.

*Cover the upper picture, and note how perfectly the lower affords the secluded atmosphere of a room; then cover the lower, and note how different is the impression produced by the upper, with its suggestion of a night sky and trees. Seeing the scenes thus, one at a time, the spectator does not recognize in either any feature of the other. But now look at both together, and see how small the actual change of the physical elements has been. The atmosphere has changed absolutely, but every structural feature is the same—the hangings, the pillars, and the steps. The transformation has entailed the placing of a lantern and flower-stand, the moving of two chairs, and the sliding back of a single panel—perhaps two minutes' work for one scene-shifter. In the use of these adaptable settings of simple elements, the great saving of time and expense over the old naturalistic method is hardly less notable than the gain in atmospheric beauty.*

*The success of this sort of setting depends upon the artist's perfect understanding of decorative design and upon a rigid economy of means. The artist in this case is Sam Hume, a young American who recognized that there was something radically wrong with practically all stage production in this country, who studied and worked in Europe for two years, with Gordon Craig among others, and who very recently made the designs for a number of productions at Harvard University. The photographs are from models for a student production of an Elizabethan tragedy. They are typical of the most advanced staging being done in the American theatre, and of the valuable experimental work being accomplished at the universities.*

And his best is significant, very significant, in the present development of American drama. But it is not great art. It is realism without the inner illuminating light of an Ibsen or a Galsworthy; and stark realism, without the poet's touch of ennobling beauty, is never universally great. Walter's plays have admirable strength, but without subtlety. They are excellent reportorial transcripts of certain brutal truths of life; but they do not give the impression of being deeply conceived: they are life itself rather than life transformed to beauty in the crucible of the writer's soul. They leave the spectator with the feeling that Eugene Walter is still the dramatic journalist rather than the dramatic seer. But he has shown a marked advance from play to play, and perhaps the next step will bring him the depth of insight and the delicacy of touch which will make him equally the forceful playwright and the penetrating artist.

Percy Mackaye, Eugene Walter, and Augustus Thomas are the dominating figures among the American playwrights. Augustus Thomas is an older man than the other two, and has travelled a more difficult road. He has had to outgrow successively the ideals of a period of successful melodrama writing, and those of a period of producing farce-comedies. When he had made his name by fashioning a long series of popular but unimportant trifles, instead of being satisfied with his success he began to realize the underlying seriousness and dignity of his art; he saw that to be lastingly worth while a play must have a theme or idea of solid value.  In his most recent work he occasionally has gone to the other extreme of preaching at his audience; having seen the need of driving home the idea, he has confused the *methods* of reaching their understanding, and has directly stated it to them in words, has preached to them—instead of making them emotionally experience a story which would carry the same conviction.  He seems not to have realized that the theatre, while it is a great moral and educative force in the life of the people, properly stimulates them to thought by suggestion rather than by statement, through emotional experience rather than intellectual understanding.  But the hopeful thing is that Thomas is a master of dialogue writing and of dramatic technique, and at the same time he recognizes the essential seriousness of his art.  If he learns to weave his theme more organically into the story, he will continue to hold a leading place on the American stage.  Even as it is, his "As a Man Thinks" is in some respects closer to the ideals of the drama of sincerity than any other American play.

Charles Klein, though not a native American, has written more plays dealing with the problems of American life than any other dramatist.  From the writing of "The District Attorney" to the writing of

"Maggie Pepper" he has treated a series of serious problems in dramas that have been immensely popular. He is generally known as the most "successful" playwright in America. And yet this is the man who is leaving for England to escape the commercial atmosphere of New York's dramatic centre. He has seen just what the critics must see: that he has lost his freshness of viewpoint in his too close connection with the business side of his profession; that he has sacrificed some of his artistic sincerity to his desire to make his plays popularly appealing. In "The Lion and the Mouse," and "The Third Degree," and "Maggie Pepper" there are touches of theatricality and of sentimentality that are entirely out of keeping with the seriousness of the themes. Klein is deeply interested in the social, political, and industrial forces of American life, and he is sincerely desirous of dramatizing them seriously; but he has a dangerous knack of fashioning pretty and sweet romances that are pleasant rather than deep. One can only thank him for waking the country to the realization of the value of American life as dramatic material, and wish him success in his attempt to regain sincerity by a change of viewpoint.

George Broadhurst is another playwright who chose a serious theme and then failed to treat it seriously. "Bought and Paid For" was a good and gripping American play, as American plays go. But it obviously was moulded to please the public, rather than to satisfy a burning desire on the author's part to dramatize sincerely and adequately a vital problem. "Comic relief" is a fine thing in serious drama when used as a foil to tragic tension. But the play leaves the impression that Broadhurst has made comic relief an end instead of a means.

Many other playwrights have fallen into the same vice of beginning with a serious theme and then drifting into farcical or melodramatic byways. Comedy treatment is legitimate always, no matter how serious the theme, but true comedy avoids the exaggeration of melodrama and the empty laughter of farce, quite as rigidly as does true tragedy. David Belasco is one of those playwrights who cannot keep clear the line dividing comedy and tragedy from farce and melodrama. His plays suffer from melodramatic and farcical turns; and often the core of drama is buried under a mass of unrelated naturalistic detail. The younger men who have worked with him necessarily have suffered from this taint of theatricality. Thus one may trace the faults as well as the virtues of Belascoism in the work of William C. DeMille. His play "The Woman" is a significant American drama in the same sense that Charles Klein's work is significant, but there is an underlying note of theatricality: it does not ring true. Certainly it does not realize the ideals of the drama of sincerity. Richard Walton Tully also collaborated with Belasco, on "The Rose of the Rancho." The result was a play with a sweet story, and characteristic richness of extraneous detail, but with the Belasco faults. Unfortunately Belasco's influence is to be detected in the recent play of Tully's sole authorship, "The Bird of Paradise." Starting with a big and serious theme, the dramatist allowed the interest to be drawn away from it by "scenic effects" and by a suggestion of theatricality in treatment. But both DeMille and Tully are of the younger generation of playwrights: they have done hardly more than their 'prentice work, and may yet write vital plays.

Edward Knoblauch's "Kismet" suffers from the same faults as "The Bird of Paradise." The production is of less value as a drama than as a spectacle. It is an interesting picture of Oriental life and customs, but the play is lost in the magnificence of the setting. And yet Knoblauch has a touch of poetry, and—if one looks back to "The Faun"—a fantastic turn, that American drama as a whole sadly lacks. It is probable, however, that he never will contribute anything essentially American to the national drama, since he so long ago expatriated himself. He is termed an English playwright almost as often as an American. In the same way Chester Bailey Fernald, author of "The Cat and the Cherub," usually is associated with the London rather than the New York theatres.

In looking for the promising names in any new
development of art, it is wise to give special attention to what the younger men are doing. In a
search for signs of the drama of sincerity in America,
two or three of the very young playwrights must be
taken into account. Edward Sheldon especially gives
promise of wide achievement. It is unfortunate,
perhaps, that lately he has cultivated the romantic
charm and rather shallow sentiment of his first play,
"Salvation Nell," instead of the wider sweep and
serious outlook of "The Nigger." His two plays
that are at present being acted, "The High Road"
and "Romance," are graceful and interesting story-
plays; but it is difficult to believe that they are
deeply significant productions, or that they will long
be remembered. But Edward Sheldon is sincere,
and he is a master of dramatic technique; moreover
he is independent and ambitious to strike into new
fields of experiment. Granting him increasing
breadth of vision, he soon should fulfill the promise
contained in "The Nigger." If he makes as much
advance in the coming ten years as Augustus Thomas
and Eugene Walter have in the past ten, his will
be a vital contribution to the American theatre.
Joseph Medill Patterson is another of the younger
men whose work probably will help to establish the
note of sincerity in American drama. A story has
gone the rounds of dramatic circles to the effect
that the touches of theatricality which mar "The

Fourth Estate" were infused during the process of popularization by "professional" playwrights, after the manuscript left the author's hands. Certainly there was in the play a suggestion of seriousness of purpose that marks its author as the thinker rather than the mere dramatic reporter. Charles Kenyon is another of the very young men to contribute seriously to the new movement. One turns to his "Kindling" as one of the most hopeful indications of the new note of truth and sincerity in American drama.

If one could properly include Charles Rann Kennedy in the group of American playwrights, his name would displace those that have been placed at the top of the list. For the author of "The Servant in the House" is a greater dramatist than Thomas, or Mackaye, or Walter, or any other of the native Americans; and his plays more closely approximate the drama of sincerity, the intensive idea-play, than those of any other playwright working on this side of the Atlantic. But in no sense is Kennedy a product of the American theatre, and however glad we may be to have him with us, we may not claim his achievement as part of the American advance.

Passing in rapid review the plays of the season of 1912-1913 in New York, one must feel that the year's contribution to the body of significant native drama is small. Edward Sheldon's new work was interesting, but less important than might justly have been hoped for. Eugene Walter's "Fine Feathers" was another of his bits of realism without poetry, which already have been discussed. "Years of Discretion" may be dismissed as a commonplace, rather than a deeply conceived, study of American life. "Peg o' My Heart" likewise may be dismissed because it is compounded of artificiality and sentimentality, owing its effectiveness to the charm of Laurette Taylor. The two remaining successes, "Within the Law" and "The Poor Little Rich Girl," are significant in contrasted ways. Bayard Veiller confesses that he wrote "Within the Law" simply to prove that he could achieve a popular success by lowering his standards. The result indicates two things: that the author is concerned with something deeper than surface aspects, and when working with serious purpose may write truthful and vital plays; and that the public now prefers melodrama dealing with serious contemporary problems to the old sort that left the mind without the least food for thought. Eleanor Gates, in "The Poor Little Rich Girl," has made a more important contribution to the American stage, because she has brought to it the note of fantasy and the touch of poetry that it so sorely needs. Her play has a certain literary distinction, and a fantastic mingling of the imaginative and the real, that are reminiscent of Barrie. And American drama does so need a Barrie!

The season as a whole is a failure when judged

by a set standard of sincerity and truth, just as the American playwright is a failure when compared with the dramatists of the English School of Sincerity. But what a success when compared with the seasons of ten or fifteen years ago! The failure is comparative only. The American stage is far from the ideal, but it is progressing in rapid strides away from its stagnation of other days.

Certainly the outlook is promising. If the lover of the theatre is discouraged at times, when he looks for actual achievement, at others he must feel a very comforting optimism. For he must sense that the time, in the theatre as elsewhere, is pregnant with great quickening forces. How fine and how beautiful the flowering may be, none of us may say. But if we are alive to all that is transpiring in the playhouse—from Broadway to the universities, and from the Atlantic to the Pacific—we cannot but feel the strength of the current of change and of progress. And if we are concerned with the growth of the drama of sincerity, we may juggle with a score of names of promise. The group whose work has been discussed, from the men of long experience in the theatre, like Percy Mackaye and Eugene Walter, to the comparative beginners, like Charles Kenyon and Eleanor Gates, surely should yield one or two dramatists worthy to stand with the world's finest. And if they fail us, there are others who may step into the front rank at any moment, whose names

have not been so much as mentioned: James
Forbes, Austin Strong, Edward Locke, A. E.
Thomas, Rachel Crothers, Edwin Davies Schoon-
maker, John Corbin, George Ade, George Bronson-
Howard, Channing Pollock, George Middleton.
Some of these playwrights have commercialized their
talents and pandered to the lower instincts of the
public; others have as yet written only plays that
are passively interesting rather than important;
others have put their hands to serious, dignified
work, but are not complete masters of their craft.
But somewhere and somehow each one has shown
a desire and an effort to contribute to vital drama.

The American playwright has developed the beginnings of a great drama, of an American drama
of sincerity.  He has touched on the surface out-
croppings of the rich mine of native material; but
he has not as yet worked with the exquisite balance
of poet and dramatic craftsman—with high purpose
and the sense of inner beauty.  In this year of our
Lord nineteen-fourteen, one can only say definitely
that he is progressing; for the rest, one may only
wait and watch and pray—and utter words of encouragement.  But brooding over all the signs, one
need not stretch the imagination too far to see emerging out of the future the man of wide vision, the
poet who yet is the perfect technician, who will weave
the material of the time into a gripping story, at

the same time revealing the beauty of his own imagination.  With that figure in mind one need not weep too copiously over the failure of the American playwright.

V

THE  NEW  STAGE-CRAFT

# THE NEW STAGE-CRAFT

The modern revolution in the playhouse has taught no more serviceable lesson than this: that the written play is only an incomplete expression of the art of the theatre—that a drama is only provisionally effective until it is actually staged. The new movement has brought a new conception of the totality of the dramatic production, of its architectonic nature. The art of the theatre exists not in the text alone, or in the acting, or in the stage decoration, but in the production *as a whole,* with play, acting and setting bound together to afford one harmonious appeal.

The mounting of the play is in a sense a separate craft; but it is a craft that exists only for the sake of the larger art—just as the craft of picture-framing may be said to exist for painting. And except in certain unusual forms of dramatic entertainment the setting has no more positive function than the picture frame.

The average playright has come to think of the writing of the play as the whole art, considering the

121

mounting a mere mechanical after-detail; the usual stage "artist" on his side has come to think of the stage setting as something entirely distinct from the play, with an independent appeal of its own. The result is that the average production tends to one of two equally inartistic extremes, as the playwright or the stage designer happens to have more to do with the staging. If the will of the former predominates the background is negligently built up, becoming a tawdry, out-at-the-elbow and down-at-the-heel affair; while if the "artist" has the upper hand the setting blossoms forth with a hundred compelling sorts of interest, not at all as an integral part of the play but as a counter-attraction to it, rich in pictorial effects and crowded with extraneous detail.

Thus contemporary play-mounting tends to the two extremes: negligence of setting and over-exaltation of setting. In the English and American theatres especially there is very little of that sort of mounting which clothes the action as a perfect gown clothes a beautiful woman—in absolute harmony with her special type of beauty, inconspicuously heightening her human loveliness rather than calling attention from it to the details of dress. The average setting is merely a shabby covering for the body of drama, or else a dress that outshines its wearer.

To understand the underlying fallacies of the ordinary sort of stage-craft it is necessary to go back to some first principles. In the first place theatre pro-

duction is an art, and is subject to those general laws
that by common agreement underlie all art.  As a
work of art, the specific production must be characterized by seriousness, by dignity, by unity, and by a
harmonious interrelation of its component parts.
Therefore there must be unity and harmony of play
and setting; the action and its background must
afford a single unified and synthetic appeal to the
spectator.  The setting must be in the *mood* of the
play.

Again, it is a first principle that dramatic art is
distinguished from the other arts by its primary dependence upon action.  The development of the
playwright's intended story, through the figures on
the stage, is the main thing.  Therefore the setting
should be so designed that it will concentrate attention on the actors rather than distract it from them.
In other words the setting should be an unobtrusive
background for the action, rather than a thing of
conspicuous beauty or ugliness that will attract
attention to itself.

The new stage-craft exists in the attempt to fit the
method of presentation perfectly to the play.  It is
embodied in the work of Gordon Craig and Max
Reinhardt and Georg Fuchs and Jacques Rouché,
and of those others who are courageously following
out their theories.  These new stage-craftsmen build
on the solid foundation of the two fundamental principles: that the setting must be an integral part of

the play and in harmony with the essential spirit
of the entire production; and that it must be unobtrusive and serve to concentrate attention on the
action.   That is the theory of their work in its
baldest statement.   In practice they attempt to carry
out these principles by suggestion rather than by
naturalistic delineation, by simple design rather than
by multiplicity and intricacy of detail, by reticence
of touch rather than by lavishness.

Before following the thought farther, it is necessary to digress for a moment and divide the field of
the new arts of the theatre, separating the forms of
production to which the new stage-craft applies from
those that are outside the usual laws of dramatic
art.   For it only too often happens that when the
student has gained a tentative understanding of the
new stage-craft—of its governing principles of harmony, of unobtrusiveness, of simplicity and suggestion—he witnesses a performance of the Russian
Ballet, for instance, that upsets every one of these
principles in his mind.   For clearly the Russian
Ballet settings are neither unobtrusive, nor simple,
nor reticent; clearly, too, this is a new art of the
theatre.   The truth is that the art that Leon Bakst
and his fellow-countrymen have created is indeed a
part of the revolution in the theatre, a protest against
the traditional conventions of the playhouse—but
it has nothing to do with the new stage-craft as that
term is generally understood.

In order to clear away this common initial confusion, to understand what distinguishes the gorgeous and lavish Ballet settings from the interpretative work of Gordon Craig and Max Reinhardt, it is necessary to strike back to the differences between the aims of the creators of the "dance-dramas" and those of the artists of the regular forms of dramatic activity. The Russian Ballet is one of the forms of art that depend first and foremost upon outward sensuous appeal, the subject-matter or story being subordinate in interest to the charm of color, movement and sound. The Russian Ballet is drama because its thread of story is expressed in action; but it depends for its effectiveness less than any other form of drama upon continuity of action, and not at all upon dialogue. It is the least dramatic of all the arts of the theatre; it has none of the built-up suspense, the tension, connoted in the latter-day use of the word "drama." It is designed merely to intoxicate the senses by a synthesis of beautiful setting, lighting, dancing and music. It ravishes the eye by beauty of color, line and movement, and ravishes the ear by beauty of sympathetic orchestration.

In this form of drama the designing of the setting is a part of the actual imaginative work of the artist of the theatre. The setting no longer is a mere background for the action, subordinate in interest to the story development, but a very real part of the art of the creator of the production. Its designing and execution are not merely interpretative; not merely a craft, but a living art, concerned with the actual creation of beauty for its own sake. Since the dramatist no longer aims to concentrate attention on the action, the setting is lifted to the position of one of the three co-ordinate elements of the synthetic whole.

With its blending of the poetry of movement, and seductive music, and beauty of line and color, to evoke a single sensuous mood of enjoyment, the Russian Ballet is indeed a fine development of theatric art. It has brought the imaginative painter into the theatre, with the painter's gorgeous palette of colors and the painter's sense of decorative line. But the very fact that the production is conceived more in the spirit of the painter than in that of the dramatist, precludes it from consideration with those forms that are more truly dramatic. The Russian Ballet, and the rich and colorful settings it has brought forth, are not the new art of the theatre, and the new stage-craft, as generally understood. The dance-drama must take its place with pure spectacle as a form to which the ordinary rules do not apply.

If, then, the reader will at this point make the mental reservation that there are certain forms of æsthetic drama, of productions of largely visual and purely sensuous appeal, to which the new stage-craft

does not pertain, he will have escaped the commonest and most confusing mistake in regard to the
revolution in stage setting.

Returning to the consideration of the ordinary
play, it should be clear by contrast that it affords
very little appeal to the eye and ear, but a very
definite appeal to the inner emotions. The spectator
is emotionally affected by succeeding incidents of
character growth; and the effectiveness depends
primarily upon continuity of action. It is to this sort
of play that the new stage-craft applies. It aims
to provide a setting that will not interrupt the all-
important action by distracting attention from the
players. Its function is unobtrusively to further the
effect the playwright intended, to frame the playwright's picture without setting up a counter-attraction, to add a suggestion of atmosphere, of mood,
without interrupting the author's dramatic design.
In this case the work of the stage setter is interpretative, rather than creative. It is less an art
than a craft; less the creation of an original beautiful picture, than a fashioning of a neutral background for the use of the dramatic artist in setting
off his action.

Approaching the theoretical aspect from another
angle, it may be said that the old method was to
leave nothing to the imagination of the audience,
while the new method is to leave everything possible
to the imagination; the old method was to create ma-

terial illusion by multiplication of naturalistic detail; the new method is to create imaginative illusion by simplification and symbolic suggestion.

In practice, how do the new stage-craftsmen achieve their ideal of imaginative illusion? How do they embody the first two principles of unobtrusiveness and harmony? Let us see how they actually carry out the theories that have been outlined.

To achieve unobtrusiveness, the new settings are designed to be just natural enough not to appear overconventional or bare, but not naturalistic enough to excite comment upon their photographic exactness. In other words, the new stage designers try to avoid on the one hand the distracting effect of what is strikingly unnatural; and on the other the disillusioning effect of what is patently a straining after naturalness.

The new artists of the theatre have learned that there is nothing in the world so unobtrusive as quiet beauty and perfect taste. So their settings are almost invariably beautiful in an unassuming way, or at least without a suggestion of bad taste. The matter of taste in designing either an indoor or an outdoor set is primarily a matter of simplicity of line and mass. To achieve a sense of completeness with the greatest economy of means, to conceive the scene in large unbroken masses, against which the actors will stand out clearly—that is the finest solution of the problem. An artist can combine a few lines and masses with a minimum of extraneous ornament and achieve a sense of richness and of satisfying pattern, where another can only achieve a bare and commonplace arrangement with the same materials. The stage revolutionists demand that the designer of settings shall have the artist's sense of design, his reticence of touch, his perfect taste. The stage-craftsman no longer can be merely a carpenter or a sign painter; he must be a "decorator" in the finest sense of the word. He must have artistic insight enough to put no unnecessary detail into his decorative composition— for such the stage setting is—and to add nothing merely "to fill space." He must avoid the bizarre, the novel, and the extreme; always he must have in mind the two ideas: beauty and unobtrusiveness.

The other requirement of the perfect setting is that it shall be in harmony with the mood of the play. Or, since every element of a work of art has its positive function, the setting in a sense must strike the keynote of the production. There is a moment after the curtain rises, and before the action begins, when the setting makes its more or less positive appeal to the audience. The average stage setter endeavors so to do his work that in that moment he will get a round of applause for the "naturalness" of the scene, or for the mechanical wonder of its invention. The new stage craftsmen in that moment after the rising of the curtain would make a quieter, inner, psychological appeal. They would have the stage suggest subtly the underlying spirit of the play, have it evoke the mood in which the action is conceived. By subconscious suggestion they subtly carry the impression that the scene is to be tragedy or comedy; with the art that conceals the means, they suggest that it is to be an intimate picture of domestic happiness, or a stark portrayal of a severe lesson of life. They do it only because they are artists and because they know the laws of pictorial or decorative composition. By proper scale, and by the proper combinations of line and mass, any atmosphere that the scene may demand can be evoked in the imagination of the audience. For example, the long, straight, upright lines bring a sense of majesty, nobility, even severity; accentuated horizontals carry a feeling of restfulness. A setting in large scale suggests tragedy; a setting on cottage scale, intimacy. So the whole range of pictorial composition is applicable to the setting that is designed to be suggestive rather than delineative, decorative rather than graphic. The new craftsmen believe that these things are more important than archæological exactness or fidelity to material detail. By the lighting, too, they suggest the mood of the production. The average theatre-goer does not realize the value of lights as an aid to emotional appeal. Unknown to

MAX REINHARDT'S PRODUCTION OF "HAMLET"

*These two photographs show the ghost scene and the grave scene as realized by Max Reinhardt. Note the absolute simplicity of the backgrounds—if they may be said to have background at all. And yet how perfectly the <u>spirit</u> of each scene is suggested, by the costuming, the lighting, and the grouping of the figures. By way of contrast call to mind the long series of tawdry, pretentious settings with which this same play "Hamlet" has been degraded in England and America.*

him his sensibilities continually are being played upon in the theatre by the changing lights.

Of course there are certain indispensable furnishings in every setting, that are called for by the action.  But the new craftsmen employ only the indispensable things.  If the play happens to call for a "period" setting, they do not go to the histories for detailed descriptions of the furnishings of the time, nor do they borrow the complete equipment from a neighboring museum.  They believe that the setting should be the result of an artist's spiritual impression of a time and place, and not the labored result of a teacher's scholarly knowledge.  Arthur Symons expressed just the thought, when he spoke of Gordon Craig's settings as having "atmosphere without locality."  Archæological exactness appeals to the historical interest, whereas the new artists of the theatre are concerned only with dramatic interest. By imaginative and suggestive impressionism they create an atmosphere that merely intensifies the dramatic action.

Before turning to actual examples of settings in the new style, it is well to inquire what changes in materials the change in stage-craft has necessitated. Not so very long ago practically all stage sets were made of painted canvas "flats."  Everything possible was painted on the cloth—sky, trees, exterior and interior walls, chimneys, mantels, doors, windows, cornices, and even chairs and tables.  Recently the box-set interior, in which only the walls are canvas, and in which the actual furniture is placed, has been adopted to a certain extent.  But almost always the cornices and similar projections are painted on, instead of actually projecting from, the walls.  One of the cardinal rules of the new stage-craft is that no projections shall be painted; for painted perspective lines are always conspicuously out of agreement with the actual floor and furniture lines, except from one point in the auditorium.  And painted shadows always noticeably fail to agree with the direction of light.

It is impossible, and unwise, entirely to eliminate canvas flats from the settings, because no other material so easily makes up into movable walls.  But such flats as are used should be painted in an unbroken tint, without attempting to delineate perspective or shadows, and without objects of any sort whatsoever painted upon them.  The new stage-craft uses flats only for interior and exterior walls, and occasionally for an impressionistic tree or background seen in obscure light.  Against these walls such projections as mantels, cornices, window sills, and steps, are built out in actual relief, thus having their own true perspective lines from every viewpoint, and casting their true shadows.  The few necessary objects on the stage, such as chairs, tables, couches, vases, are seen "in the round."  In other words, the new stage-craft uses only *plastic* materials. The few furnishings always are actually there—not merely painted there with an unnatural attempt at naturalness.

The old style exterior setting always was placed against a "backcloth," a canvas drop-curtain that usually was painted so carefully with an intricate landscape scene that the eye was very effectively carried away from the portion of the stage on which the actors appeared. To take the place of the painted back-cloth, the "cyclorama-drop" was first adopted by the new craftsmen. More recently, in a few Continental theatres, the new "cupola-horizon," or "sky-dome," has further improved the neutral background effect. In the use of both these innovations the object is to produce a background which will give the illusion of distance without drawing the eye from the foreground, where the action takes place. In both the lights are reflected upon a surface of such texture that there is merely an effect of vibrating light, without a tangible thing to attract the eye. The cupola-horizon especially gives the effect of infinite and intangible distance. Like the clear sky, it affords a cushion for the eye, an atmospheric background that is perfectly natural and absolutely inconspicuous. Against this the foreground is modeled in actual relief, and the furnishings, or properties, are shown in the round. The total effect is really a great deal more natural than the most complicated efforts of the champions of the naturalistic setting, working with the old equipment. But it must be remembered that the new artists do not follow naturalness for its own sake, but only as it furthers art. They have simply eliminated from their materials the things that are ridiculously unnatural: the flapping wings and sky-borders, the painted perspective and painted shadows, and the old wrinkled back-cloth.

In turning to some actual settings as realized by the new stage-craftsmen, it is necessary to remember that each play presents a new problem, and that there are no all-embracing rules for designing exteriors or interiors. Indeed it is to be remembered that one of the first aims of the new craft is that each background shall suggest the mood of its individual scene. And plays range from the modern so-called realistic sort, with its rigid requirements, to poetic drama, where the imagination may be given wide scope in designing the settings. But through all the examples, it is hoped, the reader will recognize the underlying principles of unobtrusiveness, of simplicity, of suggestion.

As an example of a setting showing the exterior of a church, we may take Fritz Erler's design made for a production at the Munich Art Theatre. A single heavy pillar and a pointed arch stretched halfway across the stage and ascended out of sight behind the proscenium arch. A standard holding a number of candles was placed before the arched opening—the only "property" on the entire stage. The background was merely darkness, with no tangible line or tone or light. The figures of the actors were grouped at the foot of the pillar, and all the light concentrated there. The total effect was one of singular majesty, of mystery, of solemnity. Everything was absolutely simple—but perfectly suggestive of the required atmosphere. The artist with the simplest of means led each spectator to evoke the church and its background from the imagination. The average stage designer would have attempted to show the entire façade of the church, and probably a street leading away from it on one side, with a perspective scene in the background. There would have been acres of flapping canvas flats, and myriad distorted perspective lines, and nothing to suggest the nobility of the church or the mood of this individual scene. Is there not a significant lesson in the comparison? Is it not clear that noble architectural backgrounds and wide open spaces can be brought into the theatre only by leading the spectator to imagine them?—that from the very nature of the problem, all naturalistic attempts to bring a cathedral or a mountainside within the limits of a stage setting must fail?

A second architectural setting in the new style— and one seen in America—was the palace exterior in "Sumurun." Here a flat-tinted wall, with two projections and several conventional windows and doors to break its monotony, rose from the floor and out of sight behind the proscenium, and extended off-stage to right and left. There was no need of back-cloth, of wings, of sky-borders; the one wall was the whole setting. Against it the actors stood out as they were intended to, conspicuously, like statues against a flat background. There was nothing to distract the attention from the figures; and yet, by the shapes of the windows and doors, and by the suggestive coloring, the spectator unconsciously gained the impression of an exotic, Oriental atmosphere.

A common exterior setting is a garden. The old method was to set up an elaborate display of beds of actual flowers in the foreground, with the sides bounded by "cut-cloths" of trees and foliage, and with a back-cloth depicting a vista of other palpably painted gardens. There was every sort of distracting detail effect to draw the eye away from the actors; and seldom any of the feeling of intimate seclusion and of quiet beauty that the true garden affords. The new stage-craftsmen find perhaps their most difficult problem in garden settings, because flowers and trees are among the objects most difficult to convention-alize. But they solve it far more satisfyingly than the adherents of naturalism. Most often the de-signer of the new school will clear the middle-ground and background of all the usual clutter, and of all perspective lines, by setting up a cyclorama or sky-dome, and placing against it a high garden wall. This wall—or trellis, perhaps—forms the heart of the setting, and the actors stand out from it much as they do from the "sumurun" palace exterior. The composition is completed perhaps by a few pots with flowers, set at just the right points, or perhaps by one or two conventionally-cut trees in jardinières, or even by impressionistic cut-cloths at the sides. If trees appear in the background, they are of the more conventional sorts, and rear their heads above the wall in impressionistic masses. Such garden accessories as sundials, benches, stairways, or garden-houses, often are utilized to centre the interest, but very sparingly. In this sort of background, as in architectural settings and interiors, the new stage-craft deals as far as possible in large simple masses.

Interior settings put fewer difficulties in the path of the new craftsmen, because everything already is made up of conventional lines. There are no broad sky spaces to be suggested, and no trees to be coaxed into impressionistic masses. Everything is conventionalized to a certain extent, and the problem becomes chiefly one of simplification by elimination of unessentials, and of tasteful general design. The question is how to combine the wall spaces and openings, and how to choose the furnishings, to best suggest the desired mood. Three things are practically unanimously agreed upon by the new craftsmen: first, that the doorways should not reveal other furnished rooms beyond that in which the action is progressing, and that windows should not open on detailed street scenes or landscapes—for whenever the eye is carried through the opening to something beyond, the attention is called away from the actors; second, that the wall spaces should be unbroken masses as far as possible; and third, that every unessential piece of furniture or ornament should be discarded.

For the average historical or poetic setting, for a throne-room, a palace chamber, or a banquet hall, the new artists are very likely to set up a background of heavy hangings, with perhaps a pillar on each side, against which the figures and the few pieces of furniture stand out in brilliant relief. There is no attempt at painful accuracy of historical detail, no transplanting of a museum room to the stage. It is safe to say that four-fifths of the interior scenes in Shakespeare's stageable plays would be more effective if acted against simple undecorated hangings than as now played in distractingly "realistic" settings. It is impossible to *depict* the atmospheric backgrounds that each spectator has imagined for himself in reading the plays; and only by effacing himself as far as possible, and subtly suggesting mood, can the stage setter mount Shakespeare with any approach to adequate effect. So we find Gordon Craig producing "Hamlet" at the Moscow Art Theatre with no other scenery than a series of

cream-colored screens of varying shapes and sizes,
placed in differing combinations and bathed in changing lights, to suggest the various moods and atmospheres; and in a German theatre we see the banquet
scene in "Macbeth" staged before absolutely bare
walls; and we find most of the new artists suggesting the appropriate richness of the several throne-
rooms merely by the rich texture of the simple
hangings.

In the setting for a play whose action passes in a
modern house, the designer can arrange an interior
that will be quite as satisfying in its way as the more
imaginative throne-rooms and banquet halls and
queens' chambers of poetic and historical drama.
By the exercise of perfect taste in design and arrangement; by careful attention to all those details
of scale and proportion, of height of ceiling and
placing of openings, that have a subconscious effect
on the spectator; and by the exercise of a rigid selective sense in choosing the furnishings, he can make
the modern interior harmonize with the spirit of the
play and unobtrusively heighten the mood.  As a
general rule his task is one of simplification.  The
most unobtrusive thing is the ordinary tasteful room
stripped of its unessential details.  The designer
must keep the main wall spaces as unbroken as possible, so that the action will not be lost in the intricacy of the background; and he must not fall prey
to the desire to add this touch or that just because

it is "natural." Beyond that his task is only the exercise of such artistic judgment as he might use in designing and furnishing a room in his own house. Among the finest examples of settings of this kind are those used by Japanese actors in some recent productions of Ibsen in Tokio. It is interesting to see how the Japanese have exercised their native tastefulness, and shown their realization of the value of bare spaces. Their achievement of absolutely simple but satisfying rooms is a fine contrast to the average Occidental parallel.

In the experiments that have resulted in the new stage-craft, certain simplifying devices and systems of setting have been invented. Gordon Craig has perfected a screen arrangement that promises much for the simplification of the problems of staging. He makes a series of flexible folding screens in varying sizes and shapes, and by the proper combinations can suggest all the *atmospheres* demanded by the various sorts of dramatic scenes. The screens are easily and quickly handled, unlike the usual stage equipment, and interfere less with the lighting.

Certain Continental theatres have used combinations of hangings and architectural motives, that may, with slight changes in arrangement, be made to suggest in succession the aspects of several different rooms or places. Thus the first scene of the play may call for a throne-room; the throne and a few chairs are set before hanging curtains stretched be-

# THE NEW STAGE-CRAFT

The upper picture is of an interior setting of a more or less modern atmosphere, designed by Emil Orlik for one of Max Reinhardt's productions. It illustrates the absolute simplicity and perfect taste of the best German stage-craft.

The lower photograph is of a scene in Granville Barker's production of "Twelfth Night," designed by Norman Wilkinson and A. Rothenstein. It is representative of the best staging being done in England, and illustrates especially the decorative effectiveness of colorful costumes against plastic backgrounds designed in large mass.

(The upper photograph is used by courtesy of Erich Reiss, Berlin; the lower by courtesy of the Daily Mirror Studios, London.)

tween two high columns. The next scene may be on a terrace; the throne and chairs are removed and the curtains drawn back, and the spectator looks out between the columns to an outdoor terrace where the action takes place, and to the infinite blue sky beyond, as suggestively realized in the "cupola-horizon." The third scene may be a banquet hall; curtains are dropped at the back of the terrace and it becomes a room which needs only the furnishing of table and chairs to complete the illusion. The secret of the effectiveness of this sort of setting rests in the strict economy of means, and in the perfect accentuation of the one or two decorative details. Incidentally it may be added that this method of staging is not only more satisfying to the audience than the old, but is a great deal less expensive.

The double proscenium arch, the adjustable proscenium, and the revolving stage are other inventions for simplifying or expediting the work of stage mounting, on the technical side.[1] In stage illumination the new Fortuny lighting system is a long step forward. It affords an atmospheric *enveloping* light, as contrasted with the old direct light that always *struck* the objects on the stage. It is used in conjunction with direct illumination, or alone, and promises to do away with the unnatural and inartistic footlight. The mounting of plays in the new

[1] For description of these features see the essay on theatre architecture.

style is dependent even more than the old upon
the flexibility of the lighting system, and upon the
ability of the stage electrician. So the perfecting
of the Fortuny system must be considered an important factor in the development of the new craft.

It remains only to tell who are the artists and
craftsmen who have paved the way for the revolution in stage production. Of course Gordon Craig
was the first of the pioneers in the movement. A
great deal of the confusion and the misunderstanding
that surround his work is due to the many directions of his experiments and achievements. Aside
from his service to the regular drama by reform of
setting, he has practically created, or recreated, the
mimo-drama, as exampled both in his marionette
theatre and in the wordless drama of living actors.
But those arts are outside the scope of our inquiry
into stage-craft. What is important is that Craig
first showed, by actual experiment and in his writings,
the futility of the naturalistic setting, and the value
of suggestion. He passed through successive stages,
of using only hangings, of architectural backgrounds,
and of primary dependence upon the beauty and
mystery of lights; but through it all was the refreshing quality of simplicity, and the aim of imaginative
suggestion rather than material delineation. He was
one of the first artists to point out that scenery
with painted perspective and painted shadows was
impossible artistically; and he was one of the first

to revolt against the use of footlights. The latest
development of his stage-craft is the new folding-
screen setting, that can be used more expeditiously,
with less expense, and with closer regard to the
playwright's atmospheric intent, than almost any
other of the new systems. It fails only when the
demands of the setting approach realism, as in modern social drama. Craig does not recognize the
realistic play as drama, being concerned alone with
poetic drama. Nevertheless the underlying theory
of his stage-craft, of simplicity, concentration, and
suggestion, applies almost as readily to the realistic
setting, even if his actual devices do not; and to him
the theatre owes much of the credit for reform in
mounting both sorts of drama.

Next to Gordon Craig, Max Reinhardt is the
best known of the secessionists from the regular
theatre. He followed out Craig's theories even
more energetically than Craig himself, and brought
the new stage-craft into the commercial theatre.
He is not an artist, but a director with a genius for
organization, and for calling out the best in his
helpers. In staging his plays he has been aided by
a number of well-known German designers, most
notably Emil Orlik, Ernst Stern, Ludwig von Hof-
mann, and Carl Czeschka. They have designed settings that have spread the gospel of the new stage-
craft through many countries. Their work usually
is characterized by a massive simplicity, a reliance

on imaginative suggestion, and a remarkable feeling for color. In Max Reinhardt's theatres the new stage-craft has not been limited to the staging of poetic or historical drama, but has been applied effectively to the mounting of plays of the contemporary schools. He has successfully shown that the so-called "realistic" setting—the setting that strains after naturalistic detail—is not a help but a hindrance to the realistic play. In the realistic as in the poetic drama, the play is the thing—and the setting merely a background or frame.

Georg Fuchs, of the Munich Art Theatre, stands with Reinhardt as a leader among the reformers of the German theatre. His work has been less spectacular than Reinhardt's, but none the less effective. In addition to insisting that the setting must be a mere background for the action, and in harmony with the spirit of the production, he puts great stress upon the value of an intimate relation between audience and players. With his artist co-worker and collaborator, Fritz Erler, he has realized most perfectly the aims of the "relief-theatre." The relief-theatre idea is to concentrate all attention upon the actors by making them stand out clearly from the background, to bring the actors close to the audience, and to accentuate the decorative value of the moving figures. Thus one finds that the Munich Art Theatre has a very shallow stage; the settings are very flat, and the coloring is neutral in tone; and the

actors stand out, close to the audience, like the figures in a bas-relief panel.

So many German artists have turned to the
theatre, and are practising the new stage-craft, at the
several art theatres, or the endowed theatres, or even
in the more commercial playhouses, that individual
treatment of their work is impossible.  But at least
mention must be made of Eduard Sturm, Ottomar
Starke, Knut Ström and Rochus Gliese, Heinrich
Lefler, and Karl Walser.  Some of these men occasionally overdo the decorativeness of the setting, as
several of the Russians have done; but generally
their work is of the new stage-craft in its best form.
It must be added that the German stage-decorator
works with an equipment that is far superior to that
of the average theatre of other countries.  With only
one or two exceptions, the theatres of England and
America are twenty years behind those of Germany
in stage equipment.  A German architect, Professor
Max Littmann, probably deserves more credit than
any other one man for the spread of revolutionary
ideas in stage construction.  In his many theatre
buildings he has insisted not only that the façades
and auditorium must be distinguished by dignity and
sincerity and quiet beauty, but that the stage must be
equipped with the newest devices for setting and
lighting.  Meanwhile the English and American
managers entrust their theatre building to architects
of the tinsel and gilt period, whose ideas of stage

equipment seemingly go back to the fifties and sixties.

When one looks over the field outside of Germany, one finds scattered directors and designers who are practising the new stage-craft, according to their varying abilities and their varying interpretations of the principles of simplicity and suggestion. Adolphe Appia perhaps should have been mentioned close to Gordon Craig as one of the pioneers. His idea was to displace naturalism by suggestion, but he chose to work more with the mystery of lights than with the actual settings. His experiments with figures in silhouette against backgrounds of changing lights were among the most interesting and most valuable of the beginnings of the new stage-craft. Jacques Rouché has experimented for many years at his theatre in Paris, calling in many French artists to aid him in stage design. His work follows very closely that of Craig and Reinhardt and Fuchs. In Budapest, Alexander Hevesi has been successful in introducing the new style. In Russia, Constantin Stanislavsky, of the Moscow Art Theatre, has been active in furthering the aims of the new stage art. He made the unusual and notable production of "The Blue Bird" with Egoroff's imaginative designs; and it was he who took Gordon Craig to Moscow to direct a memorable production of "Hamlet." The other Russians whose names are most often heard, Bakst, Benois, Roerich, Boris

Anisfeld, and Golovine, are concerned less with
staging plays against simple and unobtrusive backgrounds than with the creation of productions in
which the setting has a very compelling part in the
total effect, as in the Russian Ballet.

In England, Granville Barker has produced two
Shakespearean plays in settings designed by Albert
Rothenstein and Norman Wilkinson, following more
or less closely the new German standards—which,
indeed, were first derived from the work of the
Englishman, Gordon Craig.  But Gordon Craig has
not yet been afforded a chance in England to show
what his art is capable of in its perfection.  At
the Abbey Theatre, Dublin, his new screen settings
have been used effectively in poetic drama by the
Irish Players.

In the regular American theatres such plays as
have been produced in the new style have been impor-
tations.  Recently there have been welcome signs
that two New York managers, Winthrop Ames and
Arthur Hopkins, are beginning to see the light.  For
the rest, the new stage-craft in America has been
exemplified only in the experiments at the universities and in the "toy" theatres.

Such is the story of the new stage-craft.  That
it is coming—inevitably coming—the open-minded
student of the theatre cannot doubt.  With due regard to the views of Sir Beerbohm Tree and of
David Belasco, it is the *natural* way of mounting a

play, as well as the artistic way.   In its primary aim
of creating an unobtrusive background for the action,
it applies to all productions wherein "the play's the
thing."   In its more imaginative forms it is the
most beautiful mounting of the poetic drama.   Its
principles of simplification, of concentration, and of
suggestion to the subconscious faculties of the spectator, apply quite as readily to the modern realistic
drama.

In its achievement up to this time, the new stage-
craft forms the definite beginning of a complete
revolution in play-mounting.   The only ones who
cannot see it are the business men and the sign
painters who unfortunately control the great majority of theatres.   But we may be very sure that in
time art will conquer even them.   For any new mani-
festation of beauty and truth ultimately is accepted
by art-loving peoples; and its acceptance is not far
distant when such protagonists as Gordon Craig
and Max Reinhardt and Georg Fuchs are pushing
its claims.

# VI

## THE FAILURE OF THE AMERICAN PRODUCER

# THE FAILURE OF THE AMERICAN PRODUCER

When the so-called artists of the seventies and eighties were crowding imagination and beauty out of the arts of painting and sculpture, aiming futilely at a literal transcript of the surface aspects of life or sentimentalizing over its prettinesses, the art or craft of stage production naturally developed along the parallel line of unimaginative realism. But when American art began to respond to the quickening forces of American life, while the painter and the sculptor and the architect felt the call of beauty, and brought back the spiritual or poetic qualities to their arts, the man of the theatre continued unperturbed in the pursuit of photographic accuracy and naturalistic detail. So it happens that to-day the average American dramatic production is very similar to the paintings of our "tight" period, and to the sculpture of our iron-stag and painted-Indian days—but with this difference: that *nowhere in the history of the other arts is there a parallel to the present-day theatre producer's perfect realization of a false ideal.*

The story of the failure of the American producer is the story of the gradual realization of that
false ideal, under a conspiracy of commercialism
and bad taste. It is a revelation of the way of the
business man and the Philistine in the house of art.
It shows how an art may be sapped of all inner
beauty and truth, and still stand as a hollow shell
of reality, perfect in outer mechanical detail, but
quite barren of all that makes art worth while. The
American producer has followed the false gods of
naturalism and unmeaning realism until he has driven
unity and harmony from the American theatre. The
case against him may be summed up in two propositions: first, that he has produced nearly every
American drama in settings that distracted the eye
from the all-important action, destroying unity and
harmony of effect; and second, that he has introduced into every production all sorts of inorganic
incidents or "stunts," destroying the continuity of
action, and marring the author's dramatic design.

David Belasco is the arch-apostle of naturalism
in stage production, and the acknowledged leader
of American producers. He is looked up to and
imitated by the great majority of producers in the
country, and so it is not unfair to take his work for
comment in an arraignment of all his kind. With
no personal feeling against Mr. Belasco, and with
full respect for the service he has rendered to the
American theatre in certain directions, the present

writer wishes to take issue squarely with Belascoism. It is a force that has held undisputed sway in the American theatre far too long.

Unfortunately the Belasco idea has been studiously and successfully exploited before a public that is only too amiable in its acceptance of what is forced upon it with a pretense of authority. It is high time that the false stage religion be challenged, and the false principles shown forth in contrast with those of true stage art. It is worth while to set forth the Belasco creed and that of the new generation of stage artists; and then to examine some of Belasco's productions in the light of the two contrasting sets of principles.

Belasco, in a recent magazine essay, epitomized his creed in one sentence: "I believe in the little things." There one has the key to his whole method of artistic endeavor, the secret of his success and of his failure. Belasco believes in the little things; he believes that if he puts together enough little details that are "real" or "natural"—that is, true to the outer, material aspects of life—he can build a whole that will be artistically, or spiritually, true to life.

In stage setting, instead of selecting what is characteristic and casting aside what is unessential, he attempts to multiply accidental detail until he has an actual representation of nature. He leaves nothing to the imagination of the spectator. He aims, by accuracy of imitation, to create actual material illusion.

In the fashioning of the play he aims to hold the attention of the audience by bringing together a number of entertaining incidents, rather than by creating a dramatic story of sustained interest. Throughout the whole production, in play and in setting, his method is episodic and naturalistic, rather than synthetic and suggestive. He starts from the little things, and his finest accomplishment is in the little things. He is a master of detail.

The contrasting new theory of stage production is based on the fundamental artistic law that art is a thing of vision and interpretation rather than of imitation, and that unity of the whole is quite as important as perfection of the several individual parts. The new artists of the theatre argue that the literal transcript of fact is not art, but mere reporting, like topographical drawing or historical painting. They believe that the dramatic production, like every work of art, should be conceived as a whole, affording a single, complete impression. They believe that unity and harmony are the first qualities to be sought, and they are concerned with detail only as it contributes to the entire dramatic design. They believe that the play should afford a sustained appeal, without interruption through irrelevant touches of naturalism or inorganic incidents.

They conceive the setting as a mere frame for

## A BELASCO SETTING

*This photograph illustrates a setting by David Belasco, who up to this time has been generally considered the most advanced of American stage directors. It illustrates that very commendable quality of all Mr. Belasco's work, thoroughness. It is taken from the play in which he most nearly succeeded in creating atmosphere, with the inestimable help of David Warfield; and it marks the highest achievement of the naturalistic method of stage setting. Nevertheless, one cannot but feel that this sort of thing has very little to do with dramatic art.*

*Note the amount of detail in the setting—the painful accuracy with which some tasteless overcrowded room has been imitated; note the number of things placed with the one idea of arousing curiosity or drawing the interest: the furniture, the flowers, the pewter pots, the carefully labelled jars, the hats on the hatrack, the thermometer on the post, the three sets of curtains, the fussy lamp, the ashtrays and telephone and handbills on the table, and the telephone directory beneath (if your magnifying-glass is strong enough you will find that the handbills are actual circus-bills, doubtless printed for the occasion). All this is interesting—and no one ever denies that a Belasco production is entertaining. But the point is that the whole thing is fragmentary and episodic; a year afterward the spectator remembers details of the setting or action, but has entirely forgotten the play. One sometimes fancies that Mr. Belasco realizes the dramatic inadequacy of his plays, and so puts in a lot of things to please the children. That is a fine recipe for business success, but it is not art.*

*Compare this setting with that by Emil Orlik, facing page 140.*

*(By courtesy of David Belasco.)*

the action, an unobtrusive background that will not draw attention to itself by the wonder of its invention or by its conspicuous fidelity to actual life. Instead of working, as Belasco does, with a lavish hand, multiplying unimportant detail, they build up with reticent touch, out of the few most characteristic and essential elements, a simplified suggestion of the place of action. They leave everything possible to the imagination of the spectator. Their method may be summed up in a very few words: concentration by simplification and imaginative suggestion.

With the two theories in mind, let us turn to some actual interior and exterior settings designed and executed in the naturalistic method. When Belasco designs an interior setting for his play, there is hardly a square foot of wall space that is not broken up by a vase, a projection, an ornament, or what-not. A Belasco room looks as if the designer had wandered about, after the walls were set up, with a basket of "natural" objects and with an irresistible desire to stick them up on every bare spot. In making a rapid review of the settings in recent Belasco productions, it is difficult to remember one in which there was the sense of repose and of unobtrusiveness that comes from the skilful handling of unbroken lines and large unbroken masses. Belasco's first instinct is to "decorate," to destroy simplicity in a doubtful attempt at "naturalness."

It may be added parenthetically that the "realism"
that so often is connected with the names of David
Belasco and Sir Herbert Beerbohm Tree, is not the
realism of art at all, but mere naturalism—the
attempt to imitate nature in her accidental surface
aspects, and not the attempt of the artist-realist to
transfuse from life to art the deeper and more significant reality of things.   Belasco's settings are
undeniably natural; they are perfect imitations of the
real rooms of tasteless people, down to the last
unimportant detail.   All of us have wondered at the
industry and the imitative genius of the man who
could reproduce so accurately on the stage so many
details.   But has any one of us ever sensed from a
Belasco setting the intimate home atmosphere of the
domestic play, as we have in many amateur productions where there was no attempt at naturalistic
detail?   Have we ever sensed the mood of tragedy
evoked by the exceedingly simple backgrounds of the
Irish Players' productions?

In the hotel room of "The Woman," in the sani-
tarium rooms of "The Case of Becky," in the living-
rooms of "The Governor's Lady" and of "The Return of Peter Grimm" and of "Years of Discretion,"
the same faults are evident: overcrowding, over-
elaboration of detail, a lavishness that tends continually to draw the eye away from the actors.   Certainly there is in them nothing restful, nothing to
stop the eye unobtrusively and turn it back to the

action, nothing to suggest the mood subconsciously, nothing to intensify the spiritual essence of the production.   If the setting has an appeal it is to the sense of novelty, to the interest in mechanical, material detail, to the superficial interest in photographic imitation.

If overcrowding and a slavish adherence to naturalistic detail are the primary faults of Belasco's interior settings, there is one other that is almost equally destructive of sustained dramatic interest. It has become a favorite device to fit up gorgeously a second room, opening from that in which the main action is taking place, and, at a favorable moment, to open the door between, leaving the audience to gaze through, and to exclaim at the invention and naturalness of modern stage production.   Similarly a Belasco window never opens on a flat background that merely suggests the sky or a garden or a building wall, but always reveals outside a detailed landscape scene, or an intricate architectural composition.   If Belasco were an artist he would realize that whenever the eye is drawn through an opening, either door or window, away from the room in which the actors are playing, there is a definite interruption of the action: the continuity of interest is broken by the temporary excitement over something quite foreign to the matter of the play.

This revealing of a completely furnished second room, as well as the delineation of a complete per-

spective background through the windows, is merely
the adding of another "natural" detail.  But it is
more destructive to the total effect than any other,
because it draws the attention farther away from the
action, and more surely destroys concentration of interest.  There must be openings from stage rooms,
but the backgrounds which they reveal should be as
flat, as free from detail, and as neutral in tone, as
possible, if the aim of the producer is to make sustained dramatic appeal to the deeper feelings, rather
than merely scattered appeal to the surface faculties.

In interior settings Belasco is the most accomplished of all those who follow naturalness as a stage
religion.  One might examine the settings of nine-
tenths of the American producers and find the same
faults, but not carried to the same false perfection.
How many times have we seen plays set in drawing-
rooms, or artists' studios, or parlors, that were more
like college students' rooms, hung with fishnets,
trophies, and trivial tidbits of sentiment!  The
simile is not a bad one: we are indeed in the college-
room stage of theatre setting.  The sophomoric wis-
dom of our dramatic producers is reflected in almost
every Broadway production, varying in degree only
as the producer happens to have a genius for detail,
like Belasco, or merely an imitative faculty, like
so many of his followers.  If he is a Belasco he may
give us at times such a *tour de force* as the Childs
Restaurant scene of "The Governor's Lady," with

all its distracting accuracy of detail, or perhaps a completely furnished Colonial room (which should be seen only in a museum) ; but generally he will give us something overcrowded, overdetailed, and with scattered points of interest, that is both unbeautiful and unnatural, without Belasco's insinuating veneer of reality.

It is not necessary to dwell extensively upon the matter of exterior settings as designed by the American producer. They have the same faults as the interiors, though perhaps in more ridiculous measure, since it is easier to throw a veil of plausibility over an imitation of a room than to give a material illusion of out-of-doors. One remembers only too clearly the clutter of naturalistic properties; the trees that are real in the foreground, canvas "cutouts" in the middleground, and mere painted semblances of trees in the background; the buildings with real doors and windows in quaking canvas walls; the inevitable well, if it is a farm scene (and the real water that comes up in a dry bucket) ; the live horse protruding its head from the stable doorway, if there is any possible excuse for a stable; and the street scenes with their signs, their lamp-posts, and their depressingly accurate representations of the average dingy street-fronts. And occasionally there have been the river and lake scenes, with boats tossing on real water; and once a real lettuce-field that caused no end of wondering comment. But how

many outdoor settings in the American theatre can
we call to mind that unobtrusively struck the keynote
of the action, that heightened the mood of the play
by suggestion, that formed a restful background for
the all-important action?   That sort of setting alone
is worth while when one is producing drama for the
sake of drama, and not merely to entertain, like a
circus, with a series of sideshows.   The trouble is
that the simple, restful, and suggestive setting always
is part of an artist's conception of the whole production; and the American producers, from Belasco
down, may be fine naturalists or fine pictorial historians, but are not artists.

Let us turn from the settings to those incidents
that are introduced into the action, presumably with
the idea of increasing the interest, but generally with
the result of breaking the dramatic tension.   In that
essay in which Belasco makes his confession of faith
in the little things, he tells of a cat that was made
to walk across the stage and stretch itself at a
certain point in each performance of "Hearts of
Oak," and of a baby who became animated always
at just the right point of the play.   "That cat," he
writes, "was always greeted with laughter and applause, and every night brought down the house.
. . . The animated baby won the house every
night, and both the cat and the baby drew hundreds
to the theatre."   We easily can believe him, and we
can picture the spectators stopping to wonder how

the trick was accomplished.  But what of the sustained mood that had been built up if the play was
a real drama?  Was it not shattered at just the
point where the audience gave its attention and
applause to the cat and the baby?

In a current Belasco production, "The Woman,"
one of the most intense scenes is laid in a room on
the upper floor of a modern hotel.  The audience
has been brought to a point of almost breathless suspense, in the expectation that a certain character will
come up to the girl in the room.  In the midst of
this dramatic silence there is heard the peculiar
crescendo squeak of a pneumatic elevator.  The
sound is wonderfully imitated.  Invariably a rustle
runs through the audience, and almost every person
turns to his neighbor to comment on the cleverness
of the trick.  It is indeed remarkable naturalism,
and it appeals to humanity's desire for novelty, and
to its "vaudeville sense."  But in the momentary
interest in this detail, the entire sustained mood is
shattered.  When the audience again gives its attention to the story of the play, the entire built-up
dramatic interest has collapsed.

If Belasco would admit that he is not concerned
with art, he would knock every prop from under
the arguments here advanced.  If he is content to
consider that he is creating mere entertainment, like
the circus or the musical comedy, or the empty forms
of farce—productions that belong to the business

of amusement rather than to the art of the theatre—
one can have no quarrel with him for introducing
any incident or effect that he desires.  Or even if
he is content to have his work classed with such
productions as "The Old Homestead," that are little
more than sublimated vaudeville shows, wherein a
thread of story is utilized as an excuse for introducing singing, and anecdote-telling, and episodic
happenings, without regard to cumulation of dramatic interest—then one cannot quarrel with his
method of production.  But Mr. Belasco does not
admit that he is working outside the boundaries of
the legitimate art of the theatre.  Indeed, one
gathers from his essays that he believes that he is
doing a very important service to American dramatic art.  And more than once his work has been
held up before an admiring audience as the very
apotheosis of American achievement in the theatre.
But art that is serious and unified and of a certain
dignity never yet has been created by combining such
inconsequential and unrelated elements of entertainment as the stretching cat and the animated baby;
nor from any number of such mechanical wonders
as the perfect imitation of an elevator's squeak.

The recent annals of the American stage have
been full of descriptions of such remarkable naturalistic details; the clocks that struck the same hour
several minutes apart, as they would in real life;
the telephone switchboard connected with the central

office; the rainstorm of real water, falling from a network of shower-bath tubing; and (to forsake Belasco for the moment) a real linotype machine in actual operation. They all are cases of immaterial accidentals glorified to "stunts" at the expense of the spiritual essence of the plays. The moment the audience gave its attention to any one of them the illusion was destroyed, not heightened. It is as though a painter reproduced a detail in a corner of his painting so well that it continually distracted all attention from the main work and from its artistic significance.

There is one other source of distraction that only too often mars the average American production; and the producer is at least negatively responsible for it, since it should be his duty to see that nothing is allowed to interfere with the interest in the unfolding dramatic story. Why the stars—far more intelligent people than the producers—should continually overdress, forgetting every canon of reticence and taste, is a stage mystery. Some of the cheaper productions are little more than parade grounds for the latest styles in clothes. And even the so-called "first-class" productions suffer from the parading of extreme or even bizarre creations. For instance, "Bought and Paid For," which in some respects approached so near to real drama, was marred by an inexcusable exhibition of the ultra-fashionable in dress. It is safe to say that at several points everyone in the audience felt more interest in certain beautiful but very noticeable gowns than in the action of the play.  To bolster up plays of frank artificiality the introduction of such features may be allowable—anything is, for that matter—but in a drama of serious intent it is distinctly an interruption: it is not art.

Looking back over the discussion, of the exterior and interior naturalistic settings, of the introduced irrelevant incidents, of overdressing, it should be clear to the reader that there is one underlying fallacy which nullifies the entire achievement of the American producer: he misconceives the mission of art and the method of the artist.  For, after all, art is conventional and selective, affording a unified impression to the spectator; whereas the creation of the American producer is slavishly imitative, strained and episodic.  It is unnatural just to the extent of its straining after naturalness; and its appeal is primarily that of vaudeville.  It has sacrificed the imaginative element, the beauty of thought, and the typically dramatic, cumulative, emotional interest, for the superficial appeal of perfectly imitated surface detail, and of unconnected episode.

Since the productions of David Belasco have been chosen almost exclusively for comment, it is only fair to outline now his real service to the American stage.  For he does stand head and shoulders above most of his fellows, even though he has wandered

# AN AWFUL EXAMPLE

This "*awful example*" is a photograph of a throne-room as actually produced on a New York stage. When one notes the thousand and one glittering points of gilt and marble and glass, each fighting for attention, and the overpowering spaciousness of it all, one wonders what chance the actors had to dominate the setting. The eye naturally goes wandering out between the rows of columns, turns up to the over-accentuated ceiling, comes restlessly down the elaborate chandelier, drops to the fore-stage, and then is again drawn back to the maze of glittering points of interest. Concentration of attention and sustained dramatic mood are absolutely impossible in such a setting. Compare this picture with that of Sam Hume's very simple throne-room, and with those of Max Reinhardt's and Granville Barker's settings.

from the true confines of art.    In the first place,
Belasco combines to a certain extent the offices of
manager, producer, playwright, stage director, scene
designer, and electrician.    Belasco's is one of the
very few theatres in which every element of the
production goes through the hands or the mind of
one man.    And there can be no doubt that one of
the great needs of the theatre to-day is the existence
of a number of such all-commanding directors.    The
thoroughness of Belasco's work is indeed a lesson to
those other producers who blindly delegate their
duties to a dozen individual workers, thus bringing
forth a production without co-ordination.    Again, the
American theatre owes Belasco a debt for the lesson
of painstaking care which his preparation of a play
affords.    For Belasco never hurries a production.
He puts forth a very few plays each year, and he
spares neither time nor expense to make them perfect according to his standards.    Their shortcomings
mark simply the limits of his artistic ability; his
faults never are those of the managers who forever
are scrambling to get something on the stage as
quickly and as cheaply as possible.    Again Belasco
has perfected certain mechanical devices that can
be used quite as readily for artistic as for naturalistic
effects.    In lighting, especially, he has been able to
advance far beyond his American fellow-producers.
His lighting methods and lighting effects are less
important than those of certain Continental stage

artists, perhaps, only because he is concerned with producing a natural light where they seek chiefly a beautiful light or one suggestive of the mood of the action. And lastly, Belasco served the American stage by developing the box set interior to a certain solidity, by discarding the old style "flat" set for the more satisfying "plastic" sort. In other words, he discarded the most ridiculously unnatural elements of the naturalistic setting. He made the always unsatisfying naturalistic setting as satisfying as it ever can be.

Thus Belasco has accomplished much for the American theatre; but at the same time he has nullified the chief value of his service by mistaking the fundamental principles of art. He is the incomparable mechanician rather than the man of vision, the inventive genius rather than the imaginative poet. His failure as a stage artist is the more pathetic because he sees the right goal, because he wants to create an atmosphere. But he tries to accomplish it by an accurateness that is commonplace, rather than by a symbolism or a suggestion that is beautiful. He is like a man who finds the right road to his destination and then walks in the wrong direction. He describes his work as the poetic adaptation of nature; but he is constantly travelling away from poetry and into prose.

Belasco presents the spectacle of a man who is worse than his fellows only because he has been more

successful in realizing their ideals.  He is a worse
offender in naturalism only because he has arrived
at a more accurate perfection; he is a more dangerous force in the American theatre because he dis-
guises his tricks with all the outer semblance of art;
he plans an effect that is photographically natural,
and then leads up to it as to a dramatic climax,
with the most finished artistry.  Klaw and Erlanger,
or the Shuberts, or any one of a score of lesser
producers, might have yielded the examples for this
discussion.  Their settings, or at least those that they
presumably direct, have all the same strained naturalism, and their ideal embraces the same episodic
sort of action.  Their work differs from his simply
in that it lacks the disguising gloss, the insinuating
semblance of art by which he has led even discerning
critics to an acceptance of fundamentally false productions.  In England, Sir Herbert Beerbohm Tree
has achieved a similar hollow success, and deserves
to stand with Belasco himself—but that is another
story.

In summing up the failure of the American producer, it is necessary only to repeat a sentence from
the opening paragraph: his achievement is the perfect realization of a false ideal.

Forsaking the commercial producer, it is worth
while to examine the signs that point to an ultimate
revolution of stage production in America.  For outside of New York (where the entire progress in the

new stage-craft has been limited to the work of two of the younger managers) there are encouraging beginnings of a better era in the staging of plays. Two movements are chiefly concerned in the work of redeeming American production from absolute stagnation: first, the growth of the so-called experimental or art theatres; and second, the development of dramatic departments and dramatic activities at the universities.

In the experimental playhouses the most valuable work has been done at the Boston Toy Theatre and the Chicago Little Theatre. At the Toy Theatre the plays, ranging from poetic drama to the most realistic of modern drama, were staged by Livingston Platt, who put into practice the fundamental principles formulated by Gordon Craig. While modifying the Craig method according to ideas of his own, Platt has sought consistently to build up unobtrusive backgrounds, gaining atmospheric effects by simple suggestion rather than by elaborate detail. Very recently he has staged some Shakespearean plays at the larger Castle Square Theatre in Boston, and in spite of the limitations of equipment, achieved in certain scenes a very unusual success. In his productions of "The Comedy of Errors" and "Julius Cæsar" there were some very interesting combinations of hangings and columns, that were made to serve adequately with slight changes for several scenes of differing atmosphere; and the street scene in "The Comedy of Errors" and the garden scene in "Julius Cæsar" were such simple imaginative backgrounds as would have done credit to any of the more advanced Continental theatre designers. At the Chicago Little Theatre the staging has been even simpler, the background often consisting of mere hangings. Occasionally the settings have been more elaborate, creating atmosphere or mood by symbolic suggestion. But never has the aim been mere imitation of nature. Under the direction of Maurice Browne the Little Theatre designers always have worked as artists and never as naturalists or historians. In both the Toy Theatre and the Chicago Little Theatre the stage directors have exhibited those qualities that the American commercial producer so sadly lacks: good taste, reticence of touch, and concentration of effect. With similar experimental theatres and stage societies just beginning their work in a half dozen other American cities, the revolutionary gospel of simplicity and good taste promises to spread very rapidly.

At the universities the dramatic renaissance has taken the shape of revivals of plays of other times in their original settings, and occasionally the production of modern drama in experimental settings based more or less upon the new stage-craft as practised in the European art theatres. Many Greek plays have been presented, sometimes on the severely bare Greek stage, sometimes with partial concession to the modern desire for scenery, sometimes incongruously in the full mediocrity of modern "stage art." Elizabethan dramas have been played before backgrounds that left everything to the imagination of the audience, and Miracle Plays have been presented with only the crudest of stage devices and stage properties. All these productions have served to teach the younger generation of playwrights and the younger generation of playgoers how independent good drama is of all the clutter of the usual commercial setting. At least one university, Harvard, has an experimental theatre, wherein the most advanced ideas of staging are tested. Recently the Harvard Delta Upsilon Society presented "The Comedy of Errors" in simple symbolic settings designed by Gardner Hale, a student. The production, inconsequential as it was in certain respects, nevertheless was notably more artistic and truer to the spirit of the playwright than any commercial Shakespearean production seen in this country. More recently a graduate student, Sam Hume, has been creating settings that are among the finest examples of the new stage-craft in America. Hume had the benefit of two years' work under Gordon Craig in Europe, and naturally follows out Craig's progressive ideas, though not slavishly. Having had experience in acting, scene-designing, and directing, he combines, better than any other American perhaps, those abilities that Craig insists the true artist

of the theatre must have. His experiments, both in
the college theatres and in semi-professional productions in Boston, are bringing a new and very refreshing note into the American theatre.

Returning to the more professional productions,
one finds that the new stage-craft has crept into
the commercial theatre to a slight extent. Winthrop Ames has exhibited an interest in the simpler
sort of settings, not only recently at his Little
Theatre in New York, but as far back as the days
of his directorate of the New Theatre. His productions of the past two years have stamped him as the
most consistently artistic of the American directors,
though he has yet to free himself of the last traces
of traditional influence. A comparative newcomer in
the producing field, Arthur Hopkins, has presented
"Evangeline" with four of the ten settings as finely
simple and suggestive as anything in the European
theatres. Among the actors, William Faversham
has turned to the new stage-craft, rather timidly
perhaps, but with enough interest to give promise
of better settings for his future productions. Margaret Anglin was one of the first to revolt against the
inartistic naturalism of the average American production, and to recognize the beauty and fitness of
the work of the European secessionists. Her productions of Sophocles' "Antigone" and "Electra" at
the Greek Theatre at Berkeley were notable rever-
sals of all the accepted rules of the American

theatre; and more recently she has commissioned
Livingston Platt to direct the staging of her Shakespearean productions. When "Chantecleer" was
produced in America, John W. Alexander collaborated with J. Monroe Hewlett and W. H. Gilmore
in designing and executing some woodland settings
that were far above the average, but not so successful as the still simpler work of Platt and Hume and
Hopkins. At the Boston Opera House, Joseph
Urban, an Austrian artist, has designed some beautiful settings, that seem to be based on a combination of the principles of the new German stage-
craft and those of Leon Bakst and the other Russians. Some of his backgrounds have been admirably simple, and adaptable to every sort of play;
but as a rule they are conceived pictorially rather
than decoratively, and are applicable to such mixed
productions as opera rather than to pure drama—
and so are less important to the progress of American dramatic art as a whole. They are comparable
to the settings for "Boris Godounov," by the Russian artist Golovine, imported for the Metropolitan
Opera House, New York; they mark the highest
achievement in the old style pictorial background.
In the commercial theatre, too, we have had occasionally such fine examples of the new stage art as
the Reinhardt production of "Sumurun"; but they
hardly deserve mention in an essay on the American
producer, since plays and settings were imported

complete from Europe. "The Yellow Jacket" was the exceedingly rare exception to the average rule: a drama conceived poetically and staged successfully by Americans. It was a thing of great imaginative beauty—one of those fine flashes of genius that sometimes suddenly illumine the dark periods of an art.

The American stage has outgrown the exaggeration of action and thought of melodrama, but still clings to the sensationalism of scenery and stage mechanism of the ripest melodrama days. Melodrama "insisted on the obvious"—and passed with other hollow phases of drama. But the American producer continues to pursue naturalism in setting, which is merely the accentuation of the obvious in outward material detail. So the American producer has failed ignominiously. In his perfection he has become just what his false ideals would tend to make him: *the great master of unimportant detail.* The next stage in dramatic progress will be the passing of the producer as we know him—and with him will go the false gods of naturalism, of commercialism, of Belascoism. We have seen how the experimental theatres and the universities are training artists to take his place. Let us hope that their success merely will be the brighter for his failure.

# VII

# THE REAL PROGRESS OF THE AMERICAN THEATRE

# THE REAL PROGRESS OF THE AMERICAN THEATRE

## I

There is no other spot in the world which can boast of so many "first-class" theatres in so small an area as that narrow belt in New York City which is termed "Broadway." Certainly no other American city has shown a twentieth part of New York's activity in producing "shows" and in sending out travelling companies to exploit those shows. The rest of the country is indeed so barren of producing centres that it is generally known on Broadway by the vague generic name "The Road." But when one is looking for the real progress that is being made in the American theatre to-day, one turns not to Broadway but to "The Road"—not only to such cities as Chicago and Boston and Philadelphia, but to places which the New York manager probably does not even know by name: to Madison, Lake Forest, Cambridge, Carmel, Wellesley, and a dozen other towns which do not show even as pin-points on the maps of dramatic commerce.

Edwin Björkman recently explained conditions in the professional theatre in an illuminating way. He said that the American theatre was organized as a vast gambling business; and the professional gambler, he explained, is the last man in the world to take a risk. So the Broadway producer, afraid above all else to play the game in a new way, and clinging tenaciously to his traditional superstitions and conventions, repeats himself year in and year out; and New York spills to the four corners of the country an unending stream of musical comedies, and revues, and crook plays, and society farces. It is only the very rare exception that is new, that is different, that is original. Thus the professional theatre has set up a false ideal of commercial success and imitation—and real progress does not come that way.

The true progress of dramatic art in America is coming in the amateur and semi-professional theatres and dramatic societies which have sprung up in the last ten years, to satisfy a longing which the professional playhouse entirely overlooks, and as a protest against the commercialization of the regular theatre. These theatres and societies have advanced far beyond the professional playhouses because their ideal lies in the realm of dramatic art rather than of commercial success, and their methods are experimental rather than traditional and set. They have held themselves free from the conventions and artificial standards of Broadway, and they have pushed out into all sorts of new fields. They have not developed a great American drama, and they have not freed the American theatre from the inartistic faults of setting and staging and acting that have all but strangled to death whatever other drama was brought to it. But they deserve most of the credit for whatever advance has been made toward either ideal.

The experimental theatres may be divided roughly into two classes. First there are the "art" theatres, like the Chicago Little Theatre and the Boston Toy Theatre, with which may be grouped the many amateur and semi-professional societies which exist for the occasional production of plays that do not commonly appear on the commercial stage. And second there are the university and college theatres, the student dramatic activities and the occasional revivals by professional actors of classic and literary plays before academic audiences. It is here that the worldwide spirit of change is reflected in the playhouse, and it is here that there is freedom for experimentation.

The Chicago Little Theatre is perhaps the most typical "art theatre" in the country. From amateur material Maurice Browne, the organizer and director, has whipped into shape an organization which stands to-day as one of the most vital expressions of the new dramatic spirit in America. During the first season the productions ranged from Euripides' "The Trojan Women" to Strindberg's "The Stronger" and "Creditors"; from William Butler Yeats' "On Baile's Strand" and "The Shadowy Waters" to Schnitzler's "Anatol." The list bespeaks nothing if not breadth of view and courage. And these are the qualities which the commercial producer so completely and so sadly lacks. The Chicago Little Theatre tends to the literary or poetic drama, rather than to intensive social drama; and it has produced literary plays that are seldom seen on the stage elsewhere, notably the less dramatic of Yeats' work and Wilfrid Wilson Gibson's "Womenkind" and "The Ferry." The staging is designed according to the newest European ideas of simplicity and suggestion, and the settings as a whole have been remarkably successful in evoking the proper atmosphere for the action. The Little Theatre company, not content with spreading the gospel of beauty in its home city, has toured the principal dramatic centers of the East, bringing a refreshing breath of dramatic sincerity into communities that usually see nothing but the more artificial and sophisticated offerings of the commercial theatre.

The Boston Toy Theatre is very similar to the Chicago Little Theatre in its aims and in the breadth of its field. The organization is more truly an amateur one—its activities up to this time have taken place in a converted stable—but it plans to occupy soon a theatre of the "intimate" type in Boston's commercial playhouse district. There its organizers hope to maintain, for the benefit of a considerably enlarged audience, the experimental ideal, and the catholicity in choice of plays which has marked the series of productions during the first two seasons. The Toy has produced some little known American dramas; and among its "discoveries" in foreign fields are such notable plays as Angel Guimera's "Maria Rosa." But the Theatre's most important achievement, perhaps, has been in stage setting. It was the Toy that gave to Livingston Platt the opportunity to work out in practice his advanced theories of symbolic and suggestive staging. The work of this little playhouse really foreran a movement which promises to revolutionize American stage decoration. Already Mr. Platt has been called from the Toy to the commercial theatres, and already professional playhouses are beginning to adopt the new ideal of simplicity and harmony in setting—and the Belasco naturalism begins to decay. It is an example of the way in which the art theatres are building for the advanced professional theatre of the future.

The Chicago Theatre Society was one of the pioneers in the new movement in the American theatre. It is not organized as a producing society; but by guaranteeing financial success it has brought to the Chicago Fine Arts Theatre certain semi-professional

companies which otherwise could not have ventured
to compete with the purely commercial attractions.
During the season of 1912-1913 there appeared
under its auspices the Irish Players of the Abbey
Theatre, Dublin; Miss Horniman's remarkable company from her repertory theatre in Manchester; the
Hull House Players; the Coburn Players; the "Hindle Wakes" company; Winthrop Ames' production
of "Anatol"; and a specially organized company of
professional players, headed by Edith Wynne Mat-
thison, in some seldom-acted modern dramas.   The
list of plays produced during the season was remarkable for the many representative examples of
the work of the new English dramatists.   Shaw was
represented by "Candida" and "The Showing-up of
Blanco Posnet"; Galsworthy by "The Silver Box,"
"The Pigeon," and "Justice"; Arnold Bennett by
"What the Public Wants."   There were shown no
less than twenty-two plays by the Irish dramatists:
Synge, Yeats, Lady Gregory, St. John Ervine, William Boyle, T. C. Murray, Rutherford Mayne, and
Lennox Robinson.   "Hindle Wakes" by Stanley
Houghton, "Makeshifts" by Elizabeth Robins,
"Miles Dixon" by Gilbert Cannan, and "The Trag-
edy of Nan" by John Masefield were other exam-
ples of the modern intensive school.   To these must
be added three contemporary plays which seldom
had been staged before, Charles Rann Kennedy's
"The Terrible Meek" and "The Necessary Evil,"

and Granville Barker's "The Miracle." It is hardly necessary to say that no other city in America had so many chances as Chicago to see what real progress is being made in the English-speaking theatre; and nowhere else did the coming generation of playwrights have similar opportunity to see how the theatre is pushing out to new fields of life and thought for its material and to new methods of giving dramatic pleasure. The value of such organizations as the Chicago Theatre Society to the future of the American theatre can hardly be overestimated.

The theatre of the Hull House Players is no less an experimental playhouse than the Chicago Little Theatre and the Boston Toy Theatre. But the Hull House company differs from almost all others in that its ideal is more social and less purely artistic than that of the majority of experimental organizations. Acting and producing form the recreation of the players, and the constant association in artistic endeavor doubtless has meant much to the development and happiness of each member of the group. And in the choice of plays the larger social element, the humanitarian note, is noticeably emphasized. So one finds that plays of the type of Galsworthy's "Justice" and "The Pigeon" and Charles Kenyon's "Kindling" more often fill the Hull House stage than the more purely imaginative and literary dramas that are material for the art theatres. The Hull House Players have served American drama, too, by producing such sincere but little-known native plays as Joseph Medill Patterson's "By-Products" and H. K. Moderwell's "Manacles."

The art theatre movement is growing so fast that it is almost impossible to keep a record of all the playhouses and organizations concerned—and certainly it would not be profitable to attempt to describe each one in detail. Philadelphia has its Little Theatre, and the Los Angeles playhouse of the same name has just been opened, both being designed to do for their respective cities what Maurice Browne's Little Theatre is doing for Chicago. The Lake Forest Players, the "Plays and Players" society of Philadelphia, and the Forest Theatre group at Carmel, all are doing pioneer work in producing "advanced" drama, ranging from the seldom-acted classics to the 'prentice work of native playwrights. The amateur stage societies, that give only an occasional production and are without theatres of their own, are so numerous in America that an enumeration would merely be tedious. And yet it is from organizations of this sort that the Boston Toy Theatre and similar vital experimental playhouses have developed, and any one of the dilettante groups may suddenly blossom into a significant producing organization with its own theatre. At the other extreme, competing with the commercial theatres to a certain extent, there must be mentioned, as contributing vitally to the progress of dramatic art in

America, the several bands of open-air players, of which Ben Greet's company and the Coburn Players are most important, and the Drama Players of Donald Robertson, who brought a refreshing breath into the playhouse when the art theatre movement had barely started.

A New York man of the theatre, if he happens not to be one of those who impatiently wave aside all university and art theatre activities as negligible, may point with pride to Winthrop Ames' Little Theatre, saying that after all Broadway has the most notable of American art theatres. In a sense the claim is a just one. For nowhere else is the average of dramatic merit higher, or the staging more consistently artistic. But the New York Little Theatre is not a place for experiment. With its extended "runs," its high prices of admission, and its business organization, it takes rank not with the amateur and experimental playhouses, but with the professional and commercial theatres. It does not push out into untried fields, seeking new methods of creating dramatic interest, and learning through occasional failure; rather it carries into the commercial theatre field what the experimental theatres already have proved to be worth while. Its value lies not in creative experimentation, but in educating a wider audience to an appreciation of the true art of the theatre. It indicates what the American theatre may be when the new generation of playwrights and directors, which is being trained in the non-professional theatres and at the universities, comes into control of the commercial theatre; for it is the first Broadway playhouse to be directed by a man who is typically a product of the new movement.  Winthrop Ames is a graduate of Harvard University, and in a very true sense a graduate of the experimental theatre.  In New York City the nearest approach to a non-commercial producing company is the Stage Society.  It has done valuable pioneer work, but its activity has been more limited than that of similar organizations in other cities.  The Princess Theatre, devoting itself to one-act plays, in the beginning gave promise of valuable aid to American progress; but since it lately has turned to the almost exclusive pursuit of "shockers," it has proved to be a false hope.

The dramatic activities at the universities have been notable in two directions.  In the first place there have been a great many revivals, often in the original manner of staging, thus broadening the student's conception of the possibilities of the theatre, and offsetting in some measure the commercial theatre's tendency to resolve the drama to a stereotyped form.  And, in the second place, there recently has been a marked growth in the number of university courses offered in dramatic technique, with attendant experimental productions by student playwrights. The proportion of names of university graduates in the list of younger dramatists to whom the country

A CHRISTMAS PANTOMIME AT THE CHICAGO
LITTLE THEATRE

*This scene is from a mimo-drama presented at the
Chicago Little Theatre. Not only was the play wordless,
but there was no "scenery" in the accepted sense of the
word. The players acted in darkness, showing as
silhouettes against a curtain lighted from behind. This
very successful production was typical of the valuable
experimental work done by the Little Theatre Players
under the direction of Maurice Browne.*

*(By courtesy of Eugene Hutchinson and Maurice
Browne.)*

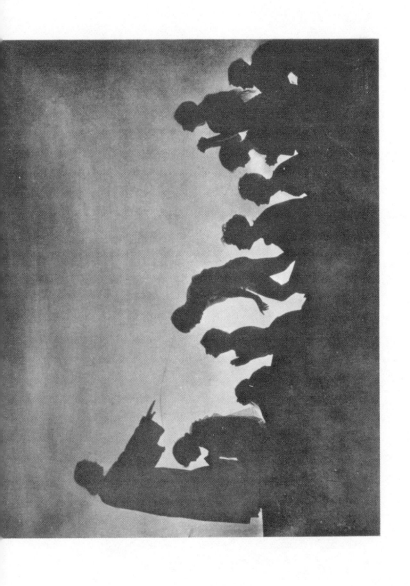

looks for its important drama of tomorrow, is sufficient indication of the value of these courses to the progress of the American theatre.

Harvard University has outstripped all others in the direction of original student composition. While its series of revivals of the older drama has been less remarkable than those of several other universities, its playwriting activity, under the unusually able direction of Professor George Pierce Baker, has been unique. Professor Baker offers a two-year course in dramatic composition, the personnel of the class being decided by a competition of original play manuscripts. In connection with the study of composition and the actual writing of the plays there has developed the "Forty-seven Workshop" (which takes its name from the number of the course), a dramatic laboratory in which the students' plays are staged and their faults practically demonstrated. Plays which are thus found worthy of public production may be staged again by the Harvard Dramatic Club, which each year offers one long play and three one-act plays by student authors. A further outlet is afforded by the Castle Square Stock Theatre in Boston, which annually produces a play by a student of Harvard or Radcliffe. The productions of the "Workshop" have ranged from pure pantomime to the deepest psychologic studies; and a single Dramatic Club bill may include a verse drama and a modern social play. To the student of practical

playwriting the value of such an experimental theatre as the "Forty-seven Worshop" is immense.
There are signs pointing to the establishment of such
dramatic laboratories at half a dozen of the leading
universities.  The Yale Dramatic Association began
many years ago to save money for the ultimate building of a "Yale Theatre," and now has a very sub-
stantial sum in hand for that purpose.

The activities at the University of California may
be taken as typical of the work of the universities
which have progressed chiefly in the direction of revivals and productions of poetic drama.  The student
organizations have been fortunate in having the
"Greek Theatre," offering unique setting for revivals
of certain sorts of classic plays.  The opportunity to
stage adequately the works of the famous Greek
dramatists was too exceptional to be overlooked.
The student productions have included "The Birds"
of Aristophanes, the "Ajax" of Sophocles, and the
"Eumenides" of Æschylus, all in Greek, and in English Sophocles' "Œdipus Tyrannus."  The English
Club, the leading dramatic organization, semi-annu-
ally produces a play in the Greek Theatre, and the
list of past productions is remarkably wide and interesting.  Of translations it includes such different
dramas as "The Little Clay Cart" from the Sanskrit, Schiller's "Maria Stuart," and Ibsen's "Vikings
at Helgeland."  Of early English drama it includes
the seldom-produced mystery play "Abraham and

Isaac," the Miracle Play "Thersytes," Dekker's "Shoemakers' Holiday," Shakespeare's "King Henry the Fifth," "The Winter's Tale," and "The Merry Wives of Windsor," and Ben Jonson's masque "The Hue and Cry after Cupid"; and of modern drama, Stephen Phillips' "Paolo and Francesca" and "Nero," Shaw's "Cæsar and Cleopatra," and Henry Van Dyke's "The House of Rimmon." Aside from the Greek Theatre productions the English Club has brought forth several important dramas, of which Alfred Noyes' "Sherwood," acted in a woodland setting, must be specially mentioned; and a second student club, "The Mask and Dagger," has produced annually modern indoor plays by Clyde Fitch, Pinero, Shaw, and other playwrights of the day. To complete the list of student activities, there have been the usual original class plays, with the usual undergraduate faults, an occasional production by the French and German clubs, and perhaps most significant of all, the truly beautiful "Partheneia," the annual dance-festival of the women students. Aside from the amateur productions at the university, the Greek Theatre has attracted professional companies in plays that could not be presented so satisfyingly anywhere else; thus Margaret Anglin has produced "Antigone" and "Electra" with all the severe beauty of the drama reflected in the dignified architectural background; Sarah Bernhardt has given a memorable production of Racine's "Phèdre"; Maude

Adams has played there in Rostand's "L'Aiglon," and in an unusually elaborate production of "As You Like It"; and Ben Greet's outdoor players have presented "Hamlet" in the complete version. Here, then, at a single university, the students have produced Greek plays and French plays, Sanskrit plays and German plays, Elizabethan drama and modern poetic drama, plays by Sophocles and Shakespeare, and plays by Pinero and Shaw, and even so-called plays by undergraduate authors; they have experimented with settings as widely varying as the bare Greek stage, the Elizabethan platform, and the modern realistic interior; and they have seen some of the greatest of modern actors in plays which never appear on the commercial stage. That this sort of dramatic education is building a splendid foundation for the coming American drama cannot for an instant be doubted. And the fine thing is, not merely that the University of California is doing these things, but that ten or twelve universities throughout the country are carrying out equally vital dramatic experiments.

Aside from the original playwriting, and the revivals and experimental productions, of which the activities at Harvard and California have been described as typical, the universities are exerting a broadening influence through the courses in dramatic literature. The instruction of such inspiring teachers as Professor William Lyon Phelps of Yale and

Professor Richard Burton of the University of Minnesota cannot help but fire the younger generation with visions of a richer and finer drama than that which fills the theatres to-day.

A comparison of the student productions at Columbia University with those of several smaller institutions suggests the interesting question of the value of a certain isolation as an incentive to original and experimental work. For the student activities at Columbia, situated in the heart of the commercial theatre centre of the country, have not been specially notable; whereas unusually interesting things have been accomplished at such comparatively isolated institutions as Dartmouth College, Stanford University, and Wellesley College. The impression of a possible commercial influence at the New York institution is strengthened when one reflects that Brander Matthews is the one among university professors who has adopted most completely the box-office standard of dramatic values. Professor Matthews has done much good by spreading a knowledge of the more practical sides of the theatre, and the dramatic museum which he has founded at Columbia is valuable on the historical side; but one must feel that the work of a man of inspiring idealism like Professor Thomas H. Dickinson of the University of Wisconsin is really a greater force for progress in the new American theatre. The growth of dramatic activities at the university at Madison is in some respects one of the most significant developments in recent theatre history. Around the university group, under the leadership of Professor Dickinson, but not composed exclusively of university people, there has grown up the association known as the Wisconsin Dramatic Society. This organization publishes a monthly magazine as well as occasional plays in book form; and it produces original plays by local dramatists, aiming at the creation of a distinctive body of Middle West American drama. Already it has constructed a small experimental open-air theatre, and plans to build a larger one when all the requirements have been amply tested; and it has paved the way for a school for the study of all branches of the art of the theatre, similar to that so long planned by Gordon Craig.

What the American theatre most needs to-day is *freedom*—freedom from traditional forms and conventional thought—freedom for experimentation. At the universities more than at any other place that freedom exists—not at the old hidebound institutions, with their set academic standards, but at the new and broader universities that are so splendidly maintaining their place at the forefront of American progress. Relieved from the necessity of commercial considerations, the university theatres have shown the ability to reach back to what is best in the greater periods of dramatic art, and the will to reach forward to untried fields. The revivals of widely varying sorts of play, showing how this master or that achieved dramatic beauty; the experiments in setting, demonstrating how independent true drama is of the gaudy trappings and distracting naturalistic details of the usual modern background; the refreshing absence of artificiality, with the physical charm of unspoiled faces and youthful figures; the teamwork acting, without stars; the student playwrights who know no better than to break all the traditional rules of form—these things are of the very essence of progress in the American theatre.

The new American drama cannot grow to vital proportions and remain independent of the professional theatre; the work which the experimental theatres are doing will not be fully effective until it reaches the larger audiences of the commercial playhouses. But the art theatre will not lower its ideals to gain that end. What must happen is this: the Broadway theatre will adopt the ideals of the art theatres. Already one may note a great advance if one compares the commercial theatre of to-day with that of five or ten years ago. While we may trace to the experimental theatres the impulses to every noticeable reform in the art, still we must see that Broadway is responding to those impulses. Five years ago the typical New York manager would have staked his fortune on the proposition that no "theorist" could "make good" on Broadway as

Winthrop Ames has done. That same manager to-day considers Winthrop Ames' theatre an exotic growth that has by chance found sustenance out of its own sphere and in an alien atmosphere. But there are some of us who feel that it is not the Little Theatre which is out of place, but the atmosphere. The next change is not for the Little Theatre to go back, but for the professional theatre to reach forward to the Little Theatre's standards. There was a time when there was only one La Follette in the United States Senate, and in those days the standpatters laughed at the suggestion that the Senate ever could be anything but a standpat stronghold; but many of the senators of that time have perforce returned to other walks of life, and the La Follette brand of progressivism pervades a large proportion of the senatorial offices. So those of us who believe in the experimental theatre look forward to a time, not far distant, when many of the standpatters of the American theatre will have graduated to other professions by public consent, a time when there will be many Winthrop Ames in the professional American playhouses. The art theatres and the universities are making that time possible.

## II

One of the most significant phases of the experimental movement is the development of the open-air theatre. Within a few years a remarkable number of so-called nature theatres have been constructed in Europe, and month by month we hear of this or that outdoor playhouse having been planned or actually built in America. The open-air theatre has become such a factor in dramatic progress, and is so full of a wholesome promise for the future that no discussion of the advance of the American theatre would be complete without at least a brief consideration of it. Certain lessons have been learned from the outdoor productions, and certain principles proved, which are of great moment to the progress of dramatic art as a whole. The experience of the Greek Theatre of the University of California may be taken as the basis for the consideration of these lessons; it is chosen not only because its story happens to be better known to the writer than that of any other, but because it is very typical of the whole open-air movement; moreover it has just completed the first decade of its existence, having antedated the majority of similar theatres in America.

The first and most important lesson learned from the open-air playhouse concerns the relation between type of play and type of theatre. At the cost of many failures it has been proved that it is worse than folly to carry into the open air what we are accustomed to consider our most dramatic types of play; it has been proved beyond a doubt that only certain simple or decorative sorts of drama can

leave the conventional built-up stage and the intimate roofed-in auditorium without greater loss than
gain.

Aside from the hygienic and economic considerations which have led to the widespread outdoor
movement in all departments of human life, the
gain in open-air dramatic production is this: a freedom from the binding sense of walls and roof, with
a consequent widening of heart and mind; a refreshing freedom from the artificial and often tawdry
conventions of commercial staging; and a largeness
of stage that permits beautiful professional effects
and decorative groupings that are impossible on the
platform shut in by "wings" and "borders." The
loss in carrying a play out-of-doors is this: the sense
of intimacy, of close absorption, can be sustained
only in the small walled-in space of the indoor theatre; subtleties of thought and vague nuances of feeling are lost in the wider open spaces; the play which
holds the indoor audience by cumulative emotional
interest, by a gripping story carried out by a few
actors with little physical movement, fails to carry
the outdoor audience because there is no longer the
feeling of being in the room with the action, no
longer the close personal interest. The intensive social drama, the purely emotional play, the play that
depends upon interior settings to create the proper
intimate atmosphere, all these it is impossible to present adequately on the open-air stage. Other and

THE GREEK THEATRE AT THE UNIVERSITY
OF CALIFORNIA

*This picture shows the stage and a part of the auditorium of the most notable of the experimental theatres of the far West. Sometimes through brilliant success, and sometimes through dismal failure, the theatre has taught many valuable lessons in regard to staging, and particularly in regard to open-air production. The structure is notable architecturally as well as dramatically; and the designer, John Galen Howard, deserves great credit for preserving the nobility of the Greek models while adapting it to modern and local needs and conditions.*

©Willard E Worden

well-known plays fail out-of-doors on account of the mechanical limitations: for here there can be no interesting scene suddenly discovered to the audience; and here there is no curtain to fall on a compelling climax; at the beginning of each act the players must enter in full view of the audience, and the action is not finished until every figure has left the stage. Plays that are specially suited to production in the open air are plays of broad rather than subtle spiritual significance, plays that hold primarily by their poetry, and, most of all, plays that depend largely upon decorative movement, upon moving processions, pageantry and dancing. The large mass, the broad sweep, the big spirit, and the shifting lines and colors, are the things that count out-of-doors.

Not only does the carrying of a play into the open limit its kind, but each open-air theatre imposes its own limitations. The Greek Theatre, with its immense stage and imposing architectural background, is uncompromising in its demands of simplicity and largeness in action and staging. The rapid volleying of question and answer, the timid voice, the delicate facial expression, all these are lost in the immensity of space. The plays that really succeed here are, first, the Greek tragedies, with the beauty of their simple stately action and their rigid economy of means reflected in the dignified, almost severe, beauty of the towering background; and second, the plays that fill the stage with a continuous decorative pattern of moving figures, with huge masses and compelling colors that are not overshadowed by the setting. When the students of the University of California decided to produce Alfred Noyes' poetic play "Sherwood," they wisely foresaw that its charm would be lost in the Greek Theatre, and presented it in a nearby wooded glade. Similarly the women students carry to an idyllic little cañon their annual "Masque of Maidenhood," which in the natural setting achieves a physical loveliness and a symbolic effectiveness that would be entirely lost on the Greek Theatre stage. There are forest and garden theatres which are ideally suited to the acting of such plays as "A Midsummer Night's Dream" and "As You Like It"; but the classic open-air theatre does not lend itself gracefully to such fantastic drama. So the open-air playhouses have taught this lesson: that production out-of-doors must be of a certain largeness and simplicity; that the type of open-air theatre definitely limits the type of drama produced, leaning on the one hand toward a classic dignity and severity, and on the other toward an idyllic loveliness; and lastly that as a general rule the pageant-like plays, the plays which delight the eye by decorative movement and color, are the most successful in the open.

The second lesson taught by the outdoor theatres is this: the average open-stage background cannot be decorated. Whether it is the stage-wall of the Greek

Theatre, with its beautifully proportioned columns and panels, or a nature theatre's background of trees and shrubs, there is little that the stage decorator can add which will not prove merely ridiculous. The keynote of outdoor staging must be simplicity; the properties must be few, and anything introduced into the setting must be massive. The failure to understand this principle has led many a commercial producer to artistic disaster. Stage managers, bringing their plays from the regular theatres into the Greek Theatre for the first time, have attempted to mask the architectural background, or at least to overcome the sense of immensity, by bringing to the stage all the clutter so dear to the commercial decorator's heart—but always they have succeeded only in showing the futility of their own artificial tricks when divorced from the artificial atmosphere of the indoor stage. In the open-air theatre it is a case of accept the natural setting or stay away. The lesson thus taught has reflected even into the regular theatre the wholesome truth that elaborate stage setting is not as important as the old-time manager would have us think; that, while it negatively can work great harm by taking attention from the play, positively it should do no more than heighten the atmosphere of the action—the more simply the better, and always with regard to imaginative rather than material illusion.

The third lesson brought out by the experience

or producing society or community that has such a theatre possesses only one half of the equipment necessary to significant and rounded series of productions.

In connection with the somewhat over-enthusiastic excitement about the outdoor theatre, it is worth while to note that the mere building of a theatre of any sort will not create a body of significant drama, or even an interest in the drama. Any theatre must be the outgrowth of a need if it is to live up fully to its possibilities. The Greek Theatre has been a success because the dramatic activity anticipated the building. For a decade before its construction an annual student play had been presented in the natural amphitheatre which the classic structure now fills, and all the student activities had outgrown the facilities at hand. Certain outdoor theatres have failed to serve any worthy purpose just because they were erected when or where the necessary interest in drama did not exist. Moreover the several types of open-air structures should be studied carefully in relation to the needs, the architectural theatre, the nature theatre, and the garden theatre each offering distinctive advantages and limitations. If the classic architectural type is chosen, the ancient models should not be slavishly followed. The Greek Theatre at Berkeley is not a true copy of a theatre of old Greece, but a theatre in Greek style and with Greek beauty conforming to modern and local requirements. The-of the open-air theatres concerns climatic conditions. It is, in short, that in any but the most favorable climates a community able to build only one theatre should make it of the indoor rather than the open-air type. The success of the productions at the Greek Theatre at the University of California has led to a rather hysterical demand at many other institutions for similar structures. But it must be remembered that the parts of California in which the Greek Theatre and the half dozen other notable Western open-air playhouses are located, enjoy a rainless season of perhaps five months, while an additional three or four months of each year are so generally fair as to practically give assurance of favorable conditions for outdoor production. In the Eastern states there can be no feeling of security that any open-air production will be given at the time scheduled. The day will probably come when the majority of universities and many experimental producing societies will have outdoor theatres; but their indoor playhouses should be built first. The climatic considerations do not afford the only argument for providing a place for indoor drama first: for we have seen that the open-air stage is suited to only a few types of drama, and those certainly not more important than the emotional and intensive types that are characteristically fitted for indoor presentation. By all means let us have as many open-air playhouses as possible, but let us not forget that a university atres may be built as archæological curiosities, but they then will have little to do with dramatic progress.

The development of the open-air theatre is even more significant in its social than in its artistic aspects. Outdoor drama is the most democratic of the arts. On the vast stages great numbers of people are brought together in a friendship cemented by a common artistic purpose. Where the commercial theatre brings together a few people in a business venture, the open-air theatre brings together many in a spontaneous and pleasurable pursuit of beauty. The citizens of those towns that have held pageants will attest to the new spirit of mutual interest which has followed the association in creating and presenting the productions. In the auditoriums, too, there is a democratic tendency that is foreign to the indoor theatre. The outdoor playhouses usually seat many more people, and the seats are not graded as excellent, good, poor, and very poor, with corresponding money values. Usually the seats are almost equally good, and the price of admission fairly low. There are no boxes from which to exhibit jewels and expensive gowns, and seldom a dividing line between a metaphoric orchestra and balcony—all of which makes for democracy.

In summary it may be said that the open-air theatre is one of the most promising influences in the dramatic world to-day. Alone it will not carry us

THE GREEK THEATRE AT POINT LOMA

*This is the unique and very beautiful "Greek Theatre" at the headquarters of the International Theosophical Society, at Point Loma, California. It is built at the head of a precipitous canyon, and faces the open sea, affording an outlook unsurpassed even by any in Greece. As the stage is open on all sides, save for the chaste little temple, the most successful productions have been pageant-like rather than intensively dramatic plays. The theatre is one of a dozen experimental playhouses in America where real progress has been made in creating new forms of dramatic art. Mme. Katherine Tingley, for whom the theatre was built, has written and directed the production here of several pageant-like plays of unusual decorative beauty and symbolic effectiveness.*

©KaThERiNE TiNgLEY

very far in the building of a great dramatic art, for
it is suited to the production of only a limited type
of play. Moreover its activity is subject to uncon-
trollable outward conditions. But on account of the
present commercialization of the regular theatres,
the outdoor drama has proved to be a stronger social
force in the community. It is in some measure an
offset to the tendency toward artificiality, and stagnation of the commercial theatre. And it affords to the
spectator a sort of satisfaction that is distinctively its
own. Properly constructed and wisely used, the
open-air theatre is a very refreshing phase, though
not the only important one, of the theatre's latter-day
progress.

# VIII

## SOME THOUGHTS ON THEATRE ARCHITECTURE

# SOME THOUGHTS ON THEATRE ARCHITECTURE

All true architects, possessing the souls of artists, must have experienced the mood of ennobling calm, even of rapturous exaltation, that comes with the witnessing of a great play. At the fall of the curtain they have sat silent for a moment in that peculiarly satisfying mood of serious spiritual contemplation which is felt elsewhere only after an inspiring service in the church. To the lover of the theatre it seems curious, and certainly very pitiable, that these artist-architects so seldom have struck this note of repose, and of detachment from the vulgarities of life, in the designing of theatre buildings.

One who cares for the art of the theatre gains from a rapid survey of the "best" American play-houses the inescapable impression that the architects have considered the theatre a dumping-ground for every form and every ornament that was too gaudy or too meaningless for other buildings. The indictment may be summed up in two general propositions: first, that they have servilely copied a general form

207

and a traditional style of playhouse—more particularly that most ornate of buildings, the Paris Opera House; and second, that in the decoration of façade and interior they have allowed their fancies to run riot, giving free play to every wild impulse to add extravagant ornament, and to cover every inch of surface with tinsel and gilt. Even the men who would not think of sticking such rubbish on public libraries, or college buildings, or churches, have "decorated" their theatres with every sort of meaningless and utterly hideous wreaths and ribbons, and Cupids, and stencilings. It is the rule rather than the exception that the American theatre (and the English, it may be added) shall be ornate, overdecorated, and vulgarly gorgeous. The average playhouse is the concrete embodiment of the "pathetic flourish." Usually it is a sort of cross between a barn and a Coney Island ginger-bread palace.

It is one of the fundamental principles of architectural design that the building shall be artistically fitted to its use; that its outward appeal to the eye shall reflect the ideals of the institution it houses. Perhaps the architects have justified their theatre buildings to themselves by thinking that they were reflecting the spirit of the current dramatic productions. They argued, perhaps, that since the world was abandoning the theatre, as an institution, to the vulgar, it was quite as well to give up its building to the vulgar. If they have, indeed, caught in

their architecture any reflection of the theatre production, it is that of the surface paint and powder,
of the tinsel and the gaudiness—and not of the essential uplifting spirit of the drama as a whole.  They
have reflected the vulgar pretentiousness and the insincerity of a passing phase of "show," rather than
the universal and lasting dignity of the true art of
the theatre.  As artists they should have been able
to see deeper.

It happens that to-day the true art is reasserting
itself in a most wholesome way.  When one speaks of
"the theatre" nowadays, one does not refer to "musical shows" and melodramatic plays, but to forms of
dramatic art that are serious, sincere, and based on
the principles which underlie all the arts.  Unfortunately musical comedies and revues, even in their
worst forms, probably will survive for many years;
but they have nothing to do with art, nor with the
theatre in the proper sense.  If one is designing the
building for a manager or producer whose whole
ideal is to gather the dollars of the tired business
man, in return for helping that unfortunate individual to digest his dinner without mental or emotional exertion—why, then by all means it should be
made as typical as possible of merely empty amusement, like a ballroom, or bar-room, or "chop-suey
palace."  If one is building a house for the prostitu-
tion of art, by all means dignity, and repose, and
chaste beauty should be avoided.  But the building

should not be confused with the theatre proper. For that is as much the temple of art as the church is of religion, or the college hall of education.

It is not necessary to inquire here into the several ways in which the new ideals of dramatic art are being realized—into the new æsthetic theatre, and the development of the drama of sincerity. It is sufficient to say that there is a very marked tightening of dramatic standards; and a very large achievement of lasting and artistic results; and finally a very definite promise of a second flowering of the art of the theatre comparable with that of the Renaissance. And through all the currents of the new movement runs the triple chord of dignity, sincerity, and beauty.

What theatres in America are adequate to house such a drama? Where can dignified plays be housed as worthily as our public collections of books are housed in the Boston Public Library and the New York Public Library, or in the hundreds of beautiful smaller library buildings scattered from one side of the country to the other? Where are there theatres as dignified and as beautiful as the buildings of our colleges, from Columbia University on the Atlantic to the University of California on the Pacific? And how many theatres are so designed that they induce a state of receptivity and foster a mood of spiritual communion, as do a hundred churches scattered from the East coast to the West?

Ah, but it is objected that there is an element of

mere amusement, or entertainment, in the theatre,
that does not distinguish the church or the college or
the library. The statement is hardly a half-truth.
The truth is that the best drama, like the best religion, and the best education, and the best book, not
only entertains, but at the same time evokes a deeper
emotional or mental response. In all of these things
entertainment is mingled with the deeper and more
significant elements. It is simply that the drama
more easily degenerates to exhibitions which merely
amuse by calling forth idle laughter or tricking to
purely momentary tears. But we do not make our
library buildings undignified just because they house
many ephemeral books designed for amusement only
—and perhaps some very frivolous ones. Even if
the circulation of fiction exceeds that of the more sub-
stantial and serious non-fiction, the architect does not
plaster overflowing cornucopias and repulsive terra
cotta Cupids over the windows of the façade, and
"decorate" the interior by adding tinseled chandeliers and spattering the ceilings with gilt sausages.
That the theatre entertains is no argument for vulgarizing it. All art entertains; that is, gives pleasure. The building should harmonize with the
dignified elements of the entertainment, with the best
that the drama has to offer.

The whole trouble is that the architects have recognized the inherent dignity of the church, the public
library, and the university, and even of the arts of

painting and sculpture, but have not realized the
serious beauty of the essential spirit of the drama.
They have visualized the theatre as a pastime, or a
business, and not as an art.

There is a close parallel between the ideal setting
for a play and the ideal playhouse. Very recently
artists of the theatre have rediscovered some of the
fundamental principles of stage decoration, which
had been buried for decades under the mass of unmeaning and distracting realism exploited by the
most "successful" managers. The principles of unity
and harmony again are finding their places on the
stage. Everything in the setting as well as in the
action is being designed to foster one single sustained
mood. The artist of the theatre is eliminating from
the setting everything that is sensational, and every
meaningless detail—every extra distracting thing
that might call the attention away from the spiritual
essence of the production; he makes his setting unobtrusive and harmonious, so that unconsciously the
spectator is put into a state of receptivity, instead of
having his attention violently drawn to this feature
or that of "the scenery."

The setting may be designed to harmonize with
the particular mood of each play, whereas the theatre
building must remain the same through tragedy or
comedy, through æsthetic drama or psychologic play.
But the principles of artistic setting apply quite as
readily to the building, though a more neutral treat-

## THE MUNICH ART THEATRE

*Note the dignity and simplicity of the exterior of this theatre. The interior is equally free from the tinsel and gilt, from the vulgarity and pretentiousness, that characterize English and American theatre buildings almost without exception. There is no intention to suggest that this playhouse and the American one shown in the following picture are to be counted among the world's masterpieces of architecture. But there is in them something of the simple beauty and nobility that make works of art more pleasing with riper acquaintance. The building shown here is by Professor Max Littmann, a German architect who has designed a remarkable series of theatres in perfect accord with the underlying dignity of dramatic art.*

ment is necessary. Almost the same words may be used of the ideal playhouse as of the ideal setting: eliminate from the architecture everything that is sensational or insincere, every meaningless detail, every unnecessary extra thing that might distract the attention; let it be unobtrusive and harmonious.

It is worth while to construct from the imagination a playhouse that will be as perfectly in accord with all serious drama as the ideal dramatic setting is with its particular play; that will help to concentrate instead of scatter the attentive faculties; that will help to make the mind and senses receptive; that will foster the spiritual mood.

In the first place it is clear that the façade will not attract the eye by gorgeousness and intricacy; but rather will satisfy it simply, with a sense of beauty and repose. The façade will be distinguished by sobriety and simplicity. There will be in it the dignity that breeds solemnity—that dignity which heretofore has been reserved almost exclusively for the church. Indeed, it seems curious that the architects have not found a hint in the fact that the drama grew out of religion, both in its first birth in the festival rites of Greece, and in its rebirth at the altar of the church in the Middle Ages. Great drama, more than any other art, has the church's inherent power of stirring men's souls to the depths; in the theatre and in the church the deeper chords of spirituality are touched as nowhere else in life. And yet how many

of the serious qualities of church architecture are to
be found in the theatre buildings of to-day?

The theatre architect, when once he has recognized
the qualities that the façade should reflect, will
quickly realize that the perfect accomplishment is
less a matter of decorating—what crimes have been
committed in the name of "decoration"!—than the
perfectly balanced combination of simple lines and
well-ordered masses.   Avoiding on the one hand the
fussy and the gaudy, and on the other the classically
cold, he will evolve from the infinite possibilities that
combination of restful lines and perfect spacing
which most exactly solves the problem at hand, and
most perfectly reflects the inner spirit of drama.

Within the theatre there will be quite as rigid
exclusion of distracting detail and unmeaning ornament as in the façade.  In the interior even more than
in the exterior it is desirable that everything shall be
designed to induce concentration rather than to scatter the attention.  A chaste simplicity in decorative
forms, and a beautiful and subtle harmony in coloring, are far more conducive to a sense of calm contemplation than a riot of unmeaning ornament and
brilliant color.  A certain richness in decoration is
not out of place within the theatre, but it should be
less the richness of profusion than that which comes
from simple forms combined with just the right
decorative touch by a master artist.  One can imagine a lyric touch in the foyer, a piece of decorative

sculpture, or a mural painting, perhaps, that would be in perfect harmony with the reposeful façade and the chastely decorative auditorium, and which at the same time would add a suggestion of the lyric element in dramatic art. But Heaven deliver us from the average "mural decorator"!

The proscenium arch always has been a favorite repository for impossible garlands, monstrous cornucopias, strings of gilt sausages, crude Cupids, half-naked women, and similar abominations. There is no other part of the theatre, within or without, that is so commonly overloaded with meaningless objects. And yet there is no place in the theatre where even passable decoration is more out of place. The proscenium frame is closer to the action than any other constructive feature of the theatre, and therefore has greater possibilities for drawing the eye away from that action. It should, therefore, be as simple, harmonious, and unobtrusive as possible. It frames the setting and action as a picture-frame does the painting. The painters are beginning to realize that nine out of ten pictures are constantly waging war with their frames for the attention of the spectator: that the usual heavy gilded frame always is tending to draw the eye away from the canvas and that there is a constant effort to keep the attention fixed: so they are very wisely beginning to adopt frames that are simple and neutral and harmonious in tone. Similarly the theatre architect must recognize that

the old style, or rather the current style, of proscenium arch, with its conspicuous ornateness, tends
to draw the eye away from the stage-picture, with a
consequent distraction of all the senses of attention.
The proscenium frame, like the picture frame, should
be simple and neutral, not calling attention to itself
by any conspicuous beauty or hideousness of its own.

The present writer has no desire to encroach upon
the prerogatives of practising architects by attempting to point out just how the various elements of
construction may be combined to produce the ideal
outward aspect he has sketched.  He does not pre-
sume to suggest how the columns, and the doorways,
the cornices and the windows, may be put together,
or the interior spaces divided and the colors combined, to produce that sense of beauty and repose
which will foster the proper mood for dramatic productions.  But he is very sure that it can be done, and
that it has been done almost ideally for other institutions than the theatre.  The realization lies with
the architect, and it would be mere presumption for
one without a life training in architecture to go into
the matter of actual design.  But it has seemed worth
while to point out the inconsistency between the architects' accomplishment and the ideals of dramatic art,
and to sketch an imaginative ideal playhouse from
the drama-lover's theoretical point of view.

But if the man of the theatre should not obtrude
his opinions about the actual combination of archi-

tectural elements, he should by all means help the architect to an understanding of certain practical requirements which the latter will have to meet only in his work for the theatre. Especially at this time of revolutionary changes behind the proscenium, the architect should know of certain developments in staging and lighting that so far have been discussed only in the most specialized of theatre publications. The architect who gained his knowledge of stage mechanism five years ago is not by that education fitted to design a theatre for the drama of to-day. And the architect who is building now without knowing of the vital changes in stage setting that are taking place in Germany, and France, and Italy, and Russia, may be very sure that his theatre will be very uncomfortably out of date and inadequate ten years from now.

The changes in settings already demand changes from the traditional sizes and shapes of stage. When the new generation of artists of the theatre began to apply the first principles of unity and harmony in their productions, they discovered that the old painted scenery, the "flats," and "wings," and "sky borders," were impossible to use artistically. They employed simple hangings to some extent; and where they retained "scenery," they began to work in "the round" instead of "the flat." That is, they began to build up actual objects on the stage, which would have their true perspective lines, differing as the

angle of sight of the spectator changed, and to discard the old method of painting perspective on canvas, in which case the lines were always "wrong"
except from one viewpoint; and instead of painting
light and shade, which never looked right from any
point of view, they used neutral masses in the background and left the built-up scenery in the foreground
to cast its natural shadows. Inevitably they needed
a stage of changed dimensions. At present, even the
least revolutionary managers are perceiving that "the
round," in one form or another, is bound to supersede the old system of painted and flapping canvas
backgrounds and borders, and foregrounds of flimsy,
illy-joined "flats." Gordon Craig has perfected a
system of folding screen scenery, which is perhaps
the most promising development of the new ideas in
setting. When one reflects that the screens form a
more artistic background for the action, that they
may be shifted for a change of scene in a small frac-
tion of the time necessary under the traditional
system, that they do not interfere with lighting from
the sides and above as did the old "flats," and lastly
that they are very much less expensive to build and
to handle, it seems clear enough that there is to be
a revolution of conditions behind the proscenium
arch. And of course there will be consequent changes
in architectural requirements. It even is possible
that there will follow a complete elimination of the

scenery loft, which always has proved architecturally troublesome.

The revolving stage is less new as a feature of the advanced playhouse.  Already it has found its way into several American theatres.  The architect should know of it, although it is doubtful whether he often will be able to convince his manager-client that its installation is worth the extra expenditure for the necessary increased ground space.  It allows three or four scenes to be set at once, one after another being swung into the proscenium opening without any resetting, thus cutting down the tiresome waits between acts to a very few minutes.  To serve the same purpose the so-called "alternate stage" system has been installed in certain European playhouses.  Two stage platforms are built on rollers.  At the end of the first act the platform with the first setting slides off to one side, and the other stage, already set for the second act, is rolled into place behind the proscenium.  Then while that act is playing the displaced platform is prepared for the third act.  A similar ingenious arrangement is that by which one stage sinks out of sight to allow another to take its place.

The architect should know, too, of the new double proscenium arch that has made its appearance in several Continental theatres.  This invention has appeared in several forms.  The first is an immovable strip of wall extending up on both sides of the stage and across the top, and built between the large outer proscenium frame and a smaller inner frame. A second form is very similar except that the top and side walls merely slide into place when the atmosphere of the play calls for a stage smaller than the outer opening would afford; the temporary inner frame thus is removable at will, while the true or outer frame is stationary. By a convention that has not yet proved its adaptability to all types of drama, the walls between the two frames usually are pierced by two doorways, one on each side, through which the actors occasionally make entrances and exits—as if they were coming from one room of the house into another, if the set is an interior, or from a house to the out-of-doors if the stage represents an exterior. A third form of improved proscenium is the flexible or adjustable arch, by which the opening can be enlarged or contracted to any desired size. It is probably the type that ultimately will be perfected and generally adopted.

The architect who designs a theatre with provision only for the older systems of stage lighting may be sure that his building will be out of date in a very few years. There can be no doubt that illumination chiefly by footlights is a passing phase, and that diffused top and side lights will take its place—with the footlight retained perhaps as a comparatively unimportant auxiliary. The Fortuny system of lighting, recently perfected in Germany, is a notable advance over all other methods, and is a revolutionary change from the illumination systems of ten years ago. Instead of the glaring direct lights, to which we have become hardened by sad experience, though hardly satisfied, the Fortuny apparatus diffuses over the stage softened light rays reflected from scientifically chosen silken bands. The result is a remarkably pleasing and unobtrusive "atmospheric" light, which *envelops* instead of *strikes* the objects on the stage. As an accompaniment of the Fortuny method of stage illumination, there has been invented the Fortuny "firmament" or horizon, a background designed to do away with the always unsatisfactory painted "back-cloth." This "horizon" is a cancave wall which is set up, or built in, at the back of the stage, with a surface of such texture that the light rays reflected against it give the effect of infinite distance. When used behind scenes "in the round" it affords the eye a perfectly neutral and restful background, without drawing attention from the foreground—as did the inevitable perspective scenes of the inartistic "back-cloth." Both the Fortuny lighting system and the "horizon" are patented improvements, which may be used only by arrangement with a German firm. But the architect who does not provide space in a theatre building for both features, or their equivalents, fails grievously in his duty to his client; for they will supersede the current systems inevitably.

There are certain evolutionary changes taking
place before the curtain as well as behind.  In regard
to both general shape and lighting of the auditorium,
there are well-defined tendencies in the "advanced"
buildings.

In the first place, there is a very noticeable tendency to discard the traditional horseshoe form of
auditorium.  The shapes in the newer Continental
theatres usually are more rectangular, and the overhanging balconies are fast being discarded.  The
pitch of the main floor is being steepened, the almost
straight rows of seats being arranged in the "amphitheatre" form—using the term in its technical rather
than its original meaning.  Both this tendency in
auditorium shaping and the development of the double proscenium may be traced back to Wagner's
theories of theatre production.  The boxes are slowly
disappearing, as is only natural; in a democratic
country especially, one can only wonder at the reten-
tion of a feature that is simply a concession to af-
fectation, and a pandering to the vanities of the
well-to-do.

In lighting the auditorium there is a very natural
and very welcome tendency to do away with the
heavy, glass bespangled chandeliers, and with the
glaring rows of unmasked lights, which so long have
outraged the sensibilities of theatregoers.  Diffused
or reflected light ultimately will replace entirely the
garish direct illumination which was the universal

THE LITTLE THEATRE, NEW YORK

*This little building, designed by H. C. Ingalls and F. B. Hoffman, Jr., is perhaps the most notable example in America of the new spirit in theatre design. Both interior and exterior show a refreshing reticence of touch and freedom from extraneous "ornament." The building houses the productions of Winthrop Ames, the most enlightened of all the directors in the "regular" American theatres.*

*(By courtesy of Winthrop Ames.)*

rule until a very few years ago; and the graduated switchboard will do away with those sudden changes from light to dark and from dark to blinding light, that are such a shock even to normal eyes. The architect who continues to design theatres with the accepted systems of auditorium lighting commits a crime against both art and public health.

Returning now from the consideration of the newer developments in practical details to the matter of the theoretical reflection of the spirit of the drama in the architecture, let us see what actual progress has been made toward the accomplishment of the ideal playhouse. In Germany, more than in any other country, the new ideas have found concrete expression. In Germany there are a number of theatres that actually are dignified, restful and harmonious throughout: that are not overdecorated and vulgarly ornate. The name of Professor Max Littmann immediately comes to mind as that of the most successful of the designers of theatres of the new type. Beginning with a form that was a close approximation to the traditional building, Professor Littmann very gradually has progressed to a style that is the very antithesis of the accepted theatre. Varying his buildings to suit the varying requirements of necessary seating capacity, kind of drama to be presented, and harmony with site and surrounding architecture, he still has managed to carry through most of his façades a simplicity, a dignity, and a sense of restfulness, that are in perfect keeping with the inmost spirit of the drama.  The little Munich Art Theatre is perhaps the one of his works that is best known to Americans, and it exhibits very satisfactorily the qualities of one phase of his art.  It is indeed a refreshing bit of restrained design, and in every way quite the opposite of the playhouses we know.  It is not to be thought that Professor Littmann and his fellows in the new movement forget the utilitarian bases of design in their passion for artistic expression.  On the contrary they meet frankly every requirement of use, letting their artistic ideal find its root in fitness to purpose.

There are other architects in Germany who are working to the same ideal, but their buildings are neither so numerous nor so generally successful as those of Professor Littmann.  And again there are those who have broken away from traditional types simply for the sake of revolt, producing theatres quite as inappropriate in their sensationalism and bizarreness as the older buildings are in their commonplaceness.

While the movement is most advanced in Germany, there is by no means a condition of stagnation in the rest of the world.  In almost every country there are a few architects who are working with the artists of the theatre to develop a type of playhouse worthy of the new drama.  Even in America there are definite beginnings of a better era in theatre architecture. In discussing the few worthy examples, we may pass by the entirely satisfying Greek Theatre of the University of California with only a word, because it is based upon the traditionally beautiful and dignified theatres of ancient Greece. The architect deserves all credit for re-creating the original beauty of the type while adapting it to modern needs, and for not modernizing (synonym for vulgarizing) its decorative features. But it is in two theatres in New York, the Little Theatre and the Maxine Elliott Theatre, that one finds the new ideals actually incorporated in so-called commercial playhouses.

In the Little Theatre there is a welcome tendency toward simplification both within and without. There still is evidence of a fear of blank spaces, an occasional tendency to break up the large masses with unnecessary decoration. But on the other hand there is a simple form of auditorium, without boxes and without overhanging balconies. There is a certain dignity and avoidance of empty pretentiousness throughout, and a gratifying absence of plush and of tinsel. It is a step in the right direction—perhaps the most notable one on this side of the Atlantic.

The façade of the Maxine Elliott Theatre is perhaps the most beautiful playhouse exterior in the country. Its quiet loveliness, its perfect restfulness, its dignified sense of decorative restraint, mark it as a building conceived in just the spirit the drama should evoke in the architect. It is a fine contrast to the thoughtless spacing and the meaningless decoration of a score of theatre façades close by.  Its interior is less satisfying than that of the Little Theatre because it is less restful, and less innocent of pretentiousness.  And one wonders how the designers of that chaste exterior could ever have brought into the building the glaring glass-bespangled chandelier that lights the auditorium.  But the total effect is so much better than the average that perhaps the critic should overlook the few defects, and only praise the understanding of the architects, and their bravery in defying the inartistic traditions of playhouse building.

The Chicago Little Theatre, hardly more than a toy playhouse, has seen fit to have its auditorium decorated with the reticence and dignity one would expect in a tasteful public library or private house.  It is a hopeful sign, since the ideals of the experimental or radical theatre of to-day are usually those of the accepted theatre of to-morrow.  Indeed there are in America a number of welcome indications of a revolt against the false conventions and vicious traditions that have strangled the art of theatre architecture for so long.

So one may dream of the coming of the day when there will be in America theatres worthy to house the drama that brings us close to a sense of the great mysteries of the human soul.  Then, when the lights are turned up after a performance, the minds that have been beguiled from distracting realities to a land of beauty will not be shocked back to an immediate realization of the vulgarity of the real world; but rather will the sensation of rapturous pleasure, and the mood of poetic wonder, be intensified by the sensuous enjoyment of the harmonious and reposeful beauty of the building.   But the ideal will be realized only when the artist-architect has dreamed that dream, and then brooded over it, and then worked with perfect understanding and with infinite patience for its embodiment in wood and steel and stone.

# IX

## ON APPLAUSE IN THE THEATRE

# ON APPLAUSE IN THE THEATRE

Of late there has been a growing conviction, among those concerned with the drama, that theatre production is properly an art. As an art its appeal is dependent upon the spectator's uninterrupted contemplation of the play, and upon the sustained mood that is evoked in the audience. Anything that tends to destroy that sustained mood is clearly a contributive cause of the failure of the art to reach its full perfection.

Gradually we are learning that in a play of serious intent it is inexcusable for the manager to introduce sensational incidents or theatrical effects that are not organic to the dramatic structure—no matter how interesting the incidents may be *per se;* and we feel that it is an impertinence in the actor to introduce individual "stunts" that are unrelated to the story or the character he is portraying; and we no longer feel grateful for the over-spectacular "scenery" and the conspicuously natural settings that distract the eye from the action. Those are some of the interruptions to our sustained mood that come from be-

hind the footlights. But now let us turn the search-
light the other way, until it shines on ourselves—the
audience—and see whether *we* cause any interruptions to the essential action, and to the sustained
mood that it is supposed to create.

Frankly now, do we not cause even more than
one-half of the interruptions during an average production? Do we not, *by applause,* clog the action,
disconcert the actors, if they are attempting to get
into the spirit of their parts, and destroy whatever
sustained mood may have taken possession of our
faculties during the preceding action? Are we not
doing more than the worst efforts of the scene painters, and more than the most bungling actor on the
stage, to destroy the illusion that is necessary to the
play's perfect appeal? It seems very stupid of us;
and yet we, collectively, go on, night after night,
clapping our boisterous way to Philistinism—drag-
ging down to vaudeville level plays that would be
works of art if produced in perfect silence.

Neither applause nor any other interruption matters in those "shows" that may be classed as belong-
ing to the business of amusement rather than to any
dignified and serious art of the theatre. The reviews, the musical comedies, the farces and bur-
lesques and melodramas, all are dependent upon
episodic appeal; there is no built-up dramatic interest
to be destroyed. So anything that the actor can
interpolate to help keep the audience in a gale of

laughter, and anything that the spectator can do to make him more pleased with himself, may be perfectly in place.   The plea for a silent auditorium applies only in the case of those productions that make pretense of being unified works of art: the comedies that bring a deeper response than mere idle laughter, the tragedies, and the so-called story-dramas.   But such plays are built with a certain climactic progression in each act, designed to hold the audience with an increasing and sustained interest; and certainly applause at any time while the curtain is up during their production is a shock to the mind that is deeply attentive.

It is worth while to follow the indictment in more detail, first as it concerns the actor, and then as it concerns the mood of the audience.

It is probable that if a poll were taken of a dozen leading actors, the resultant verdict would be against any demonstration in the auditorium before the fall of the curtain.   Doubtless thunderous applause is a gratifying tribute to the success of the actor's representation; but to the man or woman of fine sensibilities, who is attempting to get into the very mood of his or her part, it cannot but be disconcerting.   It not only breaks into the actor's preoccupation, but it destroys the delicious sense of intimacy between players and audience that comes during a drama of absorbing situations.   Applause is not necessary to the actor's understanding of the success of his in-

terpretation.   He can feel instinctively when the
audience is with him.   The breathless attention, the
subtle sense of hush that takes possession of stage
and auditorium alike, is more flattering evidence that
he has done his part perfectly than the noisiest bursts
of clapping.

The "reception" with which certain theatregoers
greet the first appearance of the play's "star"—the
round of applause that invariably comes when an
old favorite first steps upon the stage—cannot be
too severely condemned.   It is an unwarranted
thrusting of both actor and audience into the playwright's picture-frame.   In any work of dramatic
art the actor's personality should be sunk as far as
possible in the character portrayed; and the personal
opinions of the audience, on actors or any other subject, should be absolutely effaced during the time of
action.   That the "reception" is an embarrassment
to those actors and actresses who truly care for the
art of the stage, the habitual theatregoer cannot
doubt.   There always is a moment of hesitation,
while the action halts, a constrained bow perhaps,
and usually every sign of embarrassment as the actor
changes from his own personality back to that of
his part.   The actor who is saddled with an introductory reception of applause starts with a serious
handicap in gaining a sympathetic response from his
audience.   The "reception" is perhaps the most

stupid of all the audience's intrusions into the action of the play.

As to the effect of applause upon the spectator, all of us who lose ourselves in our enjoyment of the play can testify. Always when we are most deeply absorbed, when the dialogue and action have developed to that point which should be most deeply affecting, there is a sudden ripple, and then a noisy burst of clapping that brings our minds back to earth with a sickening sense of the reality of life, with a consequent collapse of all the built-up dramatic mood. The enjoyment of drama depends to a great extent upon illusion—not illusion of material detail, but of imagination. The spectator imaginatively lives through the action taking place upon the stage. The noise of applause breaks the spell absolutely. It shatters the sense of illusion, and an unpleasant consciousness of actual surroundings replaces the soul's enjoyment of an imaginative realm.

It is curious that people who would not think of applauding in the middle of a song or violin solo because they enjoyed a certain passage, will break into the wildest hand-clapping when they particularly approve a scene or a sentiment in the most affecting part of an act on the stage. They would call it a case of ill-breeding were anyone thus to break into a concert in which they had found spiritual enjoyment. Is there any reason why it is less a case of ill-breeding when the interruption comes in a serious play? Is

it any more excusable to interrupt one of the close-
knit modern dramas, in which every scene has a definite part in producing the cumulative effect, than to
similarly interrupt a musical composition, whose several "movements" certainly are no more closely re-
lated than the parts of an act of a drama? Why
should good-breeding condemn the one interruption
and condone the other? Would not a little more con-
sistency in our attitude toward the two sorts of works
of art indicate that our good-breeding is something
deeper than a blind following of what we see others
doing or not doing?

But, it is objected, surely it is permissible to show
one's approval of the play and of the acting; and, it
is asked, why should the actor now be denied his
prerogative of receiving the plaudits of his admirers
in the way in which he has been receiving them for
hundreds of years. The answer is that in so far as
the desires of the audience and the traditional privi-
leges of the actor clash with art, they must be done
away with. But there is a time for applause, that
allows the spectator freedom for the expression of
his feeling, and the actor a fitting time for receiving
that expression. Let us formulate a rule, then, as
to when applause is in place, and when out of place.
Briefly, it is that there should never be any applause
while the curtain is up, while the audience is living
in the scene and action of the play; but after the curtain has dropped at the end of the act, when the

audience has momentarily been freed from the illusion, and the actor returned to his own personality,
applause is legitimate.  But even then, if the drama
has gripped and carried the spectator, there will be
a moment of hush, an absolute stillness, after the
curtain comes down.  And some day there may be
plays so great, and audiences so delicately responsive, that there will be perfect silence in the playhouse
from the rising of the first curtain to the falling of
the last—a time when the spectator will silently
leave the theatre in that poignant mood of ennobled
detachment from worldly things that is experienced
after a particularly inspiring church service.

The church and the serious theatre are very much
alike in many respects—particularly in the depth of
their spiritual appeal.  Is it conceivable that noisy
applause after the sermon and the singing would increase the mood of abiding calm and the sense of
spiritual contemplation that the church affords?
Rather let us have more of the reverent silence of
the church in the theatre—at least while the action
is passing.

Aside from the arguments against applause on the
ground of its breaking into the sustained mood and
shattering the illusion, there are certain more practical reasons for its elimination during the play's
actual progress.  The time element must be taken
into consideration; a play often is retarded from
fifteen minutes to half an hour by the interpolated

applause.  Clearly, if it has been designed for a full
evening's entertainment, it must be shortened by that
much, or the audience kept considerably beyond the
usual time limit.  Either alternative has its serious
disadvantages.  Again, if the audience must have its
chance to greet the star with introductory applause,
the playwright must carefully arrange the entrances
for that "reception," involving an unfair restriction
on his treatment of his material.  And if there are to
be bursts of applause after the expression of every
fine sentiment, and in the midst of each particularly
affecting or pleasing scene, the dramatist must in
each case pad the following dialogue with unimportant matter, so that the audience will lose nothing
vital while the house is quieting down.  All of which
is an unwarranted twisting of a work of art to meet
the senseless demands of a thoughtless public.

The plea for the elimination of applause during
the action is not a new one.  It has been made many
times by those most deeply interested in the art of
the theatre.  Gordon Craig often has voiced his
protest against the noise of clapping in the playhouse.
And very recently, when "John Bull's Other Island"
was being presented at the Kingsway Theatre in
London, Bernard Shaw wrote an open letter to the
audiences, with a characteristic arraignment of their
rudeness in interrupting his play with clapping and
unrestrained laughter.  But the plea for the silent
auditorium cannot be made too often.  Indeed it

must be made continually until theatregoers realize its importance and heed it.

How can it be made most effectively?   Obviously neither Gordon Craig nor Bernard Shaw, nor any other writer about the drama, can reach more than a very small proportion of the theatregoing public. In only one way can the matter be brought before just those people who must be reached: through the theatre program.  When there is found one manager —or better, a group of managers—who will insert in the program a request that the audience shall refrain from any demonstration of approval until the fall of the curtain, then the movement against senseless applause will be started in earnest.   Doubtless the managers  will feel that such a request might be taken as a reflection on the intelligence and manners of the spectators.   Let it be so taken; it is no more a reflection than the now familiar request that ladies remove their hats.   It is quite as important that one shall hear the dialogue undisturbed as that one shall have an unobstructed view of the stage.   If the manager can make the one rule effective, he can quite as readily enforce the other.

Let us hope that at least one American manager will recognize to what extent the usual clapping destroys the effect of his productions, and will make the suggested prohibition.  When it once has been tried, the others will follow gradually—for it is the natural thing, and is bound to come sooner or later.

And in the meantime, let us who go often to the theatre do our part, by keeping silent when we should, and by spreading the gospel of silence whenever the opportunity offers.

Let us do our best to have more art and less noise in the playhouse.

# X

## A NEW THEORY OF THE THEATRE

# A NEW THEORY OF THE THEATRE

## I

It always is less profitable to theorize than to practise when an art is close to one's heart. And yet in the matter of the theatre, where so much energy has been spilled uselessly in weaving and unweaving conflicting theories, there is to-day more than ever before the temptation to undertake the disengaging of the tangled threads of dramatic æsthetics. For never in any art was there greater need for a sound theoretic basis of judgment than that which now exists in the field of drama. When those who should be most jealous to guard all that is vital and true in dramatic art continually are denying the badge of dramatic legitimacy to the creations alike of Gordon Craig and of Brieux, because, perforce, they do not conform to the rules of an æsthetic system formulated when mankind had developed only one of the several characteristic arts of the theatre; and when the so-called authorities are judging Leon Bakst and Bernard Shaw by the same set of principles, and

243

moreover pushing both out from the theoretic structure because they are not easily squeezed into the
moulds that were chiselled to fit Sophocles and
Shakespeare: the need for an all-embracing new
theory is painfully evident.

What recently has happened in the theatre so to
confuse the authorities is this: a few clear-sighted artists have disregarded the traditional conventions and
the old theoretical standards of the playhouse, and
have been busy creating forms of drama of which
the theorists of yesterday had not so much as
dreamed. The old boundaries have been pushed out
and the field of the arts of the theatre has been mag-
nificently widened. The actual practice has outgrown
all the accepted formulas of the old dramatic
æsthetics; and now there is nothing for the theorists
to do but accept the fact and reconsider their principles in the light of the new achievement. But so
far no one of them has regained his perspective sufficiently to map out the much-needed new basis.

There is no more barren work for the lover and
student of the drama than pursuing the sophistries
of the learned æstheticians. When one begins to
wander in philosophical jungles and metaphysical
wastes, the human joy is gone out of art. So the
present writer has no intention of trying to solve
the subtle problems of æsthetic readjustment implied
in the recent enormous advance of theatric and dramatic art. Nor does he pretend that any hard-and-

fast set of principles can serve as a foundation for actual practice; for vital art grows out of independent experiment and not from conformance to rule. But it is worth while to attempt to build up an explicit new theory that will serve as a guide for the student, indicating simply and untechnically the distinctive characteristics of the several dramatic arts. Only thus can a clear basis be established for judging the significance of the new movement in the theatre, and especially of those forms, typically artistic and typically theatric, that are outside the bounds of the old criticism.

## II

It is necessary first to re-establish the outside limits of the activities of the theatre and of drama. It is a common mistake to consider that there is only one true dramatic art, which is equally the typical art of the theatre. In truth there are several legitimate arts of the theatre, each yielding its peculiar sort of artistic pleasure; and, while all the forms that now are fully developed are dramatic in some measure, it is necessary to recognize that certain ones are more characteristically *dramatic* and others more typically *theatric*. The failure to understand this distinction has rendered invalid most of the judgment and criticism of the new achievement in the theatre.

In order to build sound new definitions of theatric

and dramatic art it is necessary to go back to the derivative meanings of the terms. "Theatre" originally meant merely "a place for seeing"; and "drama" originally meant simply "that which is done." Both definitions imply *action* as the one essential quality; and indeed every later definition either of the theatre or of drama emphasizes the element of action. But the special point that so seldom has been remarked before, and yet is so important in the light of recent progress, is this: that there clearly is a difference as well as a likeness implied in the two definitions; that in the one case the word "seeing" suggests primarily visible, or physical, action, in the sense of *movement;* while in the other the expression, "that which is done," suggests something accomplished, in the sense of *development*—as for instance story-development, or character-development.

While it still is impossible to isolate an art of the theatre that is not to some extent dramatic, it is not at all impossible to conceive of one: an art visually effective, but without a suspicion of cumulative dramatic growth; and while we now may use the terms "arts of the theatre" and "dramatic arts" interchangeably, it is profitable to make the distinction between the arts that are more typically theatric, that is, more dependent upon the visual appeal of movement, and those that are more typically dramatic, that is, dependent upon an inner development or growth. We shall find, too, this further difference: that in the one case the elements which the artist emphasizes, aside from action, also are visual, as line and mass, color, and light and shadow; whereas in the other case the necessary visual elements (necessary because action of any sort must have background or setting) are subordinated, and spoken words become a very important part of the means employed by the artist—language being the most expeditious aid to the development of human relationships.

In bringing out the importance of words as one of the primary means employed in the dramatic arts of the second sort, it is necessary to guard against the misconception of "beautiful" language as a primary aim in drama. For spoken words are rightly but a method of developing action in the theatre, and are not of the essence of drama as they are of literature. Beautiful language is rather to be considered as bearing the relation to drama that beautiful color bears to painting. By this reservation one avoids the false assumption, which has persisted from the time of the Greeks to the present day, that the arts of the theatre are merely a department of literature, or poetry.

Our conception of the theatre, then, is to be of an art which is essentially based upon action, and entirely separate from literature though borrowing a certain beauty from that art; our wider definition of action including that which is of the nature of movement, implying a more theatric form of drama, and that which is of the nature of development, implying a more truly dramatic sort of drama. And whether we personally take the greater delight in productions that tend to the one extreme, or to the other, or in those which belong to the middle ground, we may not deny to the other sorts their legitimate place in any all-embracing theory of the theatre; we may only say that the special artistic pleasure afforded by the one form is more, or less, attuned to our own responsive faculties.

## III

There are certain activities of the theatre which, though usually included in the wider definition of art, are so inconsequential that they may be left out of any consideration of what is vital drama. All art entertains; but the pleasure it affords is entertainment in a higher sense than mere amusement. Those harmless pastimes that often are accepted by an indulgent public as real dramatic art, but that do not give the peculiarly serious sort of pleasure of the higher forms of art, may fairly be set aside as mere indifferent offshoots of the parent theatre; and it is only with the latter that a theory of the theatre need concern itself.

Thus the field may be cleared by setting aside:

First, *farce;* because pure farce has only a surface appeal, being content to evoke idle laughter; it is amusement pure and simple: a form that approaches art only as it attains to comedy characteristics. Second, *melodrama;* for melodrama is merely the raw material of art, untouched by the magic of poetic conception or poetic treatment; it is tragedy that has approached the ridiculous instead of the sublime, tricking the spectator into an empty sort of emotional response. Third, *musical comedies,* and *revues,* and *"shows";* for these are bastard forms of theatre entertainment that are frankly episodic and inconsequential, appealing to the lower senses and even to the sex instincts; and though they may have a gloss of art, they never afford a sustained contemplative pleasure. And fourth, *vaudeville;* for a vaudeville production is not a distinct form, but a heterogeneous grouping of several miniature productions, one or two of which may be typically artistic, but still without potentiality to lend dignity to the whole; vaudeville, like the circus, is in its total aspect essentially inartistic, a mere commercial corruption of art. These several sorts of entertainment may be grouped as pertaining to the business of amusement; and as such they conveniently may be considered as having nothing to do with the arts of the theatre in that higher sense in which we conceive of art as a thing of seriousness, dignity and completeness.

The field under consideration may further be cleared by setting aside opera; for although opera is clearly dramatic in structure, it is a bastard form, with an inheritance more musical than dramatic. Its primary appeal is that of its music; and it may helpfully be omitted from the present discussion as one of the arts of music rather than of drama.

The true art of the theatre or of drama embraces the remaining sorts of play: the tragedy, the comedy, and that middle sort which is neither the one nor the other but partakes of the serious qualities of both—that the French call *drame,* and that we who speak English label merely "drama" for lack of a more precise generic term. These are the activities of the theatre that are "serious, complete, and of a certain magnitude," and that are characterized, like all art, by unity and harmony of parts.

## IV

In attempting to differentiate the several forms of serious art into easily recognizable groups, and in that way to arrive at a basis for judging the characteristic significance of each of the newer forms, the most natural test is that of the dramatist's emphasis on this or that element of his material. Three dramatists may take the same general material and, not only by that intangible personal something which the artist adds, but by a differing conception of the importance of this or that element, arrive at results widely varying in their ways of appeal. Thus the same dramatic skeleton may underlie a sensuous production of the Russian Ballet and a thought-provoking drama by Shaw; the same story-plot may form the basis of a gripping intensive drama by Ibsen and a loosely-joined extensive play by Shakespeare; the real differences being attributable to the divergent emphasis on material used. The differences in modes of emphasis may be inferred most easily from the dual conception of action: first the emphasis on physical, or outward, beauties, corresponding to the conception of action as visual movement; and second, the emphasis on story-development or character growth, corresponding to the conception of action as mere development.

It is impossible to isolate the method of expression entirely from the subject. The ultimate ideal of the adherents of "art for art's sake," an abstract art or abstract beauty, is impossible to realize. Certainly no artist has succeeded in creating a form without content, a method of artistic appeal without subject. But there is a beauty of outward means of expression which is distinct fram the thing expressed though not entirely separable from it; and emphasis upon it will create drama distinct in kind from that which exists primarily for the subject. And when

one considers subject in drama one may easily dis-
criminate between the subject that is primarily a
surface story of outward relationships and the subject that exists primarily for a clash of inner forces
or the development of underlying ideas—affording
an additional distinction between subject-story and
subject-idea or theme. Mindful of the three ideas
thus developed we may venture a tentative classification according to emphasis: first, the drama that
emphasizes outward beauty of form; second, the
drama that emphasizes story for its own sake; and
third, the drama that emphasizes pervading idea or
theme.

This new triple alignment of the forms of serious
drama, while deducible primarily from the new conception of the meaning of action, also agrees more
closely than any other with the commonly accepted
conception of the methods of appeal in art. All
art affords pleasure of three sorts: first, the sensuous pleasure of the contemplation of beauty; second,
emotional pleasure, through experiencing the inner
feelings that the artist has expressed in story; and
third, intellectual pleasure: the thoughtful after-en-
joyment that is in addition to the pleasure of sensuous impression and the pleasure of emotional experience, the enjoyment of a second meaning that is
over and above that appearing on the face of the
action. It is clear how closely these three sorts of
pleasure to be derived from drama correspond in

kind to the three modes of emphasis already enumerated. With the two tests—the one verifying the
other—we surely have a sufficient basis for dividing
the field of the arts of the theatre into three definite groups. These may be termed illuminatingly:
first, the *æsthetic drama;* second, the *drama of emotion;* and third, the *drama of thought.*

The æsthetic drama includes all those arts of
the theatre which emphasize primarily the outward
beauties of form, of movement, of line and mass,
of light, and even of sound—these being the typically theatric arts, that appeal primarily to the
senses. The drama of emotion includes those dramatic activities in which the emphasis is chiefly on
story-development, appealing primarily to the emotions, and yielding the pleasure of deep emotional
experience. The drama of thought includes the
forms in which the emphasis is on underlying idea
or theme, yielding both the pleasure of emotional
response and an additional intellectual enjoyment.
There is no art of the theatre that may not fairly be
placed in one of the groups or another. Indeed
the classification seems so logical that one wonders
why commentators have not made it before.

V

It is a part of the arrogance of the artist, and
perhaps a part of his necessary implicit belief in his
own individual method that he should consider the
form he creates the only true art, impatiently wav-
ing aside all others as false to the prime artistic
principles. Thus Gordon Craig may arrogate art
to the first group, insisting that it rightly is concerned only with the creation of the beauty that
appeals to the senses and through the senses to the
imagination, at the same time vigorously denounc-
ing as sacrilege any attempt to bring the artistic
activities close to life or into the service of humanity;
whereas Tolstoy may deny the name of art to that
which is merely sensuously beautiful, claiming that
it affords at best merely an anæsthetic form of pleasure, and reserving the name of true art for those
activities that not only move men deeply, but bring
them into truer and more sympathetic relationship
with each other.   But may not we, the great theatregoing public, be more tolerant?   May not we, the
lovers of art in all its forms, well be content to widen
our definition to include every creation of the artist
that gives pleasure in any of the three ways?   We
know that mere sight and sound may bring us the
healing sense of beauty; we have experienced the
peculiar joy of living through a dramatic story; our

minds have caught some gleam of a deeper order of truths underlying a story; and we know that all of these pleasures seldom have come to us except through an artist's interpretation of life. So while we may profitably study the unique power of producing beauty or pleasure that is resident in each kind, we shall do well not to limit the arts of the theatre or any of the other arts to any one of the three groups.

In examining in turn the æsthetic drama, the drama of emotion, and the drama of thought, noting the peculiar characteristics of each, it is necessary to remember that the differences are chiefly in emphasis and not in qualities that absolutely dominate or are absolutely lacking in each form. While it is easier to treat of extremes for clearness' sake, there must be the mental reservation that no one production is pure æsthetic drama, or pure drama of emotion, or pure drama of thought, but that the groups intertwine. It must be kept in mind that there always is a marriage of form and matter: that there always is at least a faint subject-interest; and that on the other hand, while the emotions and intellect are being addressed the senses very surely feel a corresponding beauty of impression in some small measure. And the preserving of this pervading harmony of appeal, even while emphasizing one element and subordinating the others, should be a jealous regard of every dramatist.

## VI

The æsthetic drama, it has been said, is the drama of emphasis on outward form, which appeals primarily to the senses. It is the art of the theatre in which the method of expression counts for more than the thing expressed. Beauty of form is lifted above beauty of content. There is very little subject-interest, and the subject usually is removed from actuality. The whole emphasis is on visual aspects, on the decorative value of movement, of line and mass and color.

It is the art of the theatre that tends to the purely æsthetic, in the old narrow sense in which "æsthetic" meant that which appeals merely to the senses. It tends to "art for art's sake," to an art in which it is impossible to distinguish subject from form. It is removed as far as possible from the literary arts, and approaches close to music, where subject or theme is most nearly indistinguis'able from outward expression. The closest parallel in the field of graphic art is the Japanese print, which affords pleasurable sensation almost exclusively by "the creative handling of pure line and color," the subject being inconsequential alike to artist and to spectator.

The method of appeal of the æsthetic drama is purely sensuous. The eye is addressed, and not the er otions or the intellect. Often there is the sym-

## AN OPERA SETTING BY JOSEPH URBAN

*This is an example of a type of the new setting that is not adaptable to pure drama, but is well suited to opera, wherein the dramatic action is only of secondary importance. The decorative grouping, the plastic setting, and the dependence upon lighting for atmospheric effects, are all of the new stage-craft; but the new simplicity has given way to an elaboration of ornament and multiplication of detail that would "kill" the ordinary dramatic production. The scene is from a production at the Boston Opera House, where Joseph Urban, an Austrian artist, has been designing settings that are far in advance of those at any other American opera house.*

pathetic accompaniment of music, affording a concurrent appeal to the ear.  The effect is impressionistic, creating mood, not thought.  In its finest forms
the æsthetic drama may reach through the senses
to the imagination, liberating the spectator from the
tyranny of the world and bringing a sweet sense of
remoteness from the urgency and commonplaceness
of human life.  In its most poignant moments its
effect is that of ravishing music: an intangible exaltation, a soul experience that, having passed, cannot
readily be described in words.

The æsthetic drama is vital art if it is vitally
important that the drama should lift the spectator
from the region of practical life to a region of
dreamy enchantment.  It bears the audience away
from the world's realities, but never invites to a
contemplation of the deeper truths of life and the
everlasting mysteries of the human heart and soul.
It is valuable because it affords a refuge from the
inherent vulgarities of every-day surroundings; but
is not of deep human significance because it generally is hardly more than a tickling of the surface
senses.  It is pre-eminently the drama of exquisite refinement of feeling; it is not at all the drama of
trenchant after-thought.  It may act as a blessed
anæsthetic to the mind; but it never stirs the soul,
never stimulates fine impulses.  Its greatest virtue
and its most grievous fault are expressed in this: that
it is the art of sensuous enchantment.

It always is illuminating to place the theory beside the concrete example.  Perhaps the truest examples of æsthetic drama are the arts that Gordon Craig has so largely created or re-created: the marionette drama and the mimo-drama of living actors.  In both forms the appeal is almost entirely visual and sensuous, the appeal of moving figures in fluctuating patterns, of sinuous line and harmonious color, of insinuating lights and subtle shadows.  The dance-drama, of which the Russian Ballet is typical, is a form of æsthetic drama in which the appeal is purely to the senses but to the ear as well as to the eye. It approaches closer to opera than does either the marionette drama or the mimo-drama.  By beauty of movement, of line and mass and color, and by beauty of sound, it affords a synthetic appeal that is at once visual and oral.  Spectacle, in so far as it ever exists for its own sake, and not in a drama of another sort (thus affording only part of a divided interest), is typical visual art, and typically an æsthetic art of the theatre.  In all of these examples it is noticeable that the materials do not include spoken words; for there is no surer way to subordinate sub-ject-interest, or literary interest, and to carry the spectator out of every-day life, than by leaving out language from the materials.  These are the activi-ties of the theatre that are most typically theatric and least dramatic.  An absolute preciseness of terms would necessitate calling them the arts of the theatre

rather than the arts of drama. But the generic
term "æsthetic drama" and the individual names
"dance-drama" and "mimo-drama" give weight to
the popular precedent of confusing "theatre" and
"drama" as synonyms.


## VII

The drama of emotion has been described as the
drama that appeals primarily by story-development
or character-development to the emotions. Its emphasis is on story for its own sake, on character-
plot working out to emotional climax. Its essence
is action, not in the sense of movement, but in the
sense of development. It interests by the changing
relationships of the characters; it is the art of soul-
crises. It is the literary rather than the visual art
of the theatre, in that the development comes chiefly
by dialogue; and literary beauty may increase its
attractiveness, much as a piece of lace may be em-
broidered into a woman's dress, adding a sort of
extraneous beauty but not disturbing the unity and
effectiveness of the whole.

The drama of emotion is a contrast to the æsthetic drama in that beauty of form is subordinated
to truth to character. The outward appeal to the
eye and ear is merely a very small aid to the effectiveness of the whole; the appeal is indeed through

"sense-avenues," but the senses are utilized not as ultimate aims but as mere carriers to the inner emotions.

The drama of emotion affords enjoyment by actual emotional experience. The spectator in effect lives through the action represented on the stage. The faculties are not lifted away from human activities but are plunged to the very heart of human life, are brought into direct contact with its inner truths and spiritual essences. As there always is some measure of mental reaction from any deep emotional stimulus, the drama of emotion is very closely allied to the drama of thought; it remains the drama of emotion only when the artist is concerned primarily with evoking the greatest possible emotional response, irrespective of any potential mental reaction.

The drama of emotion is valuable because it beguiles the faculties not indeed away from reality, but to a deeper realization of the beauty and goodness of life. It purges the mind, and leaves the spectator better fortified for his task of living. And it breeds sympathy, the most humanizing of all forces. It is not characterized by the exquisite refinement of feeling of the æsthetic drama, and it does not stir the finer impulses as does the drama of thought, but it does good in the world by yielding a peculiarly sympathetic and clarifying sort of enjoyment.

On the other hand the drama of emotion presents to the dramatist the constant danger of falling into artistic insincerity. There is a sort of dramatic trickery, bringing a false sort of emotional response, into which the form easily degenerates. The dangerous facility of the master of "the well-made play" may thus bring forth an empty dramatic shell that is without the informing light of the true artist's conception, and is unredeemed by any literary distinction, but which tricks the emotions into a momentary response.

The drama of emotion may be found in its most characteristic phase in the plays of Arthur Pinero. Here is a dramatist who confessedly sets out with no other thought than to evoke from his audience the greatest possible emotional response. He has succeeded in accomplishing his aim more unequivocably, perhaps, than any other dramatist has succeeded in realizing this or any other dramatic ideal. It is difficult to conceive of an audience leaving a Pinero play in that mood of dreamy enchantment, of poetic wonder, that might be evoked by a faultless æsthetic drama; nor is it easy to believe that the audience would feel any deep social conviction, that they would go away to brood through the night "with a divine discontent," that might indeed become an instigation to action—as they might after a drama of thought. The spectator leaves a Pinero play with the consciousness of having lived through emotional experiences that he has met elsewhere only at the one or two moments that we call the crises of life; he has been face to face with certain deeply affecting phases of life, and he has come forth with his inner self purged, and with a sympathetic feeling toward other men.   Henry Arthur Jones is only less successful than Arthur Pinero in achieving the ideal of the emotional drama, and both are merely the English followers of the French school that apotheosized the well-made play.   The drama of emotion as illustrated in the plays of Pinero and Jones is in a sense the truest of the typically dramatic arts.   It is the truest *drama* because its very essence is action, development, the actual working out of destinies.   It is less the typical art of the theatre because the visual appeal is only incidental.

## VIII

The drama of thought is emotional drama with the emphasis transferred to underlying theme, appealing to the emotions and through them to the intellect.   It is necessary to interpolate the statement that there is no such thing as a purely intellectual art; for as soon as the intellect is directly addressed, the activity becomes argument or dialectic or something equally didactic and innocent of the sensuous and emotional pleasures peculiar to art.   But art may appeal very powerfully, though indirectly, to the intellect.

In the drama of thought story-development is emphasized not for its own sake but as illustrating theme. Character growth is emphasized as typical of social truth. The play is not developed primarily for a big scene, for the sole end of a strongly emotional climax, but for a burning idea, for social passion.

The spectator lives through the story, and having returned to reality after the emotional experience, finds that there is a remainder of thought. Through some illuminating inner light hidden behind the surface story he unconsciously has received a message. The drama of thought is the drama that is rich in second meaning. It evokes a lingering mood of serious contemplation that lasts far beyond the actual passing of the story. Through the remaining contemplative mood, the reflective after-thought, it often becomes an incentive to action. Thus it has an indirect ultimate aim of betterment, and in the hands of genius may become a social force as potentially corrective as the church or the school.

The drama of thought has been miscalled the ethical drama. It is ultimately ethical, but the name suggests an immediate pointing out of a specific moral that is quite outside the province of art. Dramatic art never states directly to the intellect, never teaches didactically, never attempts to speak with a show of authority. But as the emotions and the moral consciousness are close together, there is the indirect moral impulse that arises from feeling deeply and understanding subjectively some moral maladjustment of life—all drama being concerned more or less with such maladjustments. The deep emotional experience merely clears the way to moral understanding; it purges away the prejudices and selfishnesses that ordinarily imprison the thinking, actively moral part of man.

If the æsthetic drama easily slips into a form that merely tickles the senses, and if the drama of emotion easily descends to tricking the emotions into a false and empty response, the drama of thought spreads before the playwright a network of dangers even more difficult to avoid. Because the drama of thought tends to become an intensive study of contemporary life, because it usually is very close to the people's problems, there is the constant temptation to show forth actual segments of life that are emotionally compelling in a mean way, but that are not transformed to art by the artist's informing light. Again there is the danger, already shadowed forth, of slipping over into dialectic. Because the drama of thought is so clearly a social force, it is easy to distort it to mere propaganda, completely losing sight of the sensuous and emotional elements, leaving only something dry and didactic and lifeless, like a sermon or a school lesson. Again, be-

cause the drama of thought tends to become inti-
mately introspective, turning the full light into the
dark corners of both individual and social life, that
heretofore have been peeped into only timidly or
secretly, there is the danger of choosing the material
just because it is dark, of baring brutally wounds
that should be shown forth only with the reticent
touch of art; and finally of excusing sensational exhibitions of corrupt or corrupting phases of life by an
immoral sort of tag-end morality.

That the dramatists of thought and their incompetent imitators slip into these errors is not, however, argument against the validity of the form.
At its best the drama of thought is the most completely satisfying, the most human, and the most
social of the arts of the theatre. If one of its masters strikes down through the unbeautiful aspects of
living it is only to reveal to us more clearly the
beauty of the universal foundations of life—and
one should judge an art only by the masters.

The drama of thought is typically the drama of
to-day. At no previous time have the intellectual
message and the social significance of art been so
emphasized as in the works of contemporary playwrights. The Greek tragedians developed a form
of drama in which the theme was perfectly clothed
in emotional story, and they achieved a compactness
of form, an economy of means, that was not approached again before Ibsen. But it remained for

the dramatists of the past two decades to resolve the type to its quintessential form. Ibsen, the dramatist of profound thought; Björnson; Hauptmann in his earlier plays; Galsworthy; Brieux at his most dramatic; and Shaw, who is the master of the comedy of thought, when the dramatist is not lost in the propagandist: these are the typical figures in the field of the drama of thought. A brief mental review of the significant work of these men should sufficiently verify for the reader the theoretical description of the group, without further discussion. Especially it should be clear what is meant by the "second meaning" which is over and above that appearing upon the face of the action.

Before turning from the drama of thought it is well to define a term which has gained considerable currency as identifying those forms of dramatic activity which lie opposite to the æsthetic drama. The *psychologic drama* is a name that includes both the drama of emotion and the drama of thought in contradistinction to the æsthetic drama. It is a term which identifies, rather clumsily, the activities of the theatre that are more typically dramatic as distinguished from those that are more typically theatric or more purely æsthetic. It doubtless had its origin in the conception of the modern dramatic movement as a thing chiefly concerned with character-development, prying deeper into life, as contrasted with the drama of mere surface appeal. But even though it implies an unwarranted limitation, it must be used as the most satisfactory name for the drama of emotion and the drama of thought as one generic group.

## IX

In summary this may be said: the new theory of the theatre widens the field to include all those activities that are characterized by the serious qualities of art, that are either typically theatric or typically dramatic: that is, distinguished on the one hand by action in the sense of decorative movement, or on the other by action in the sense of development.

From this new dual conception of action may be deduced a new alignment of dramatic forms: first, the æsthetic drama, which includes the more typically theatric or visual forms; those that have a primarily sensuous appeal; and second, the psychologic drama, which includes the more typically dramatic forms, that appeal by story-development to the inner faculties; the psychologic drama being further divisible into the drama of emotion and the drama of thought, according to the dramatist's emphasis upon story-growth for its own sake or upon the development of underlying idea.  Not only does the triple alignment thus made, of æsthetic drama, the drama of emotion, and the drama of thought,

agree with the new conception of the dual nature
of action, but it falls in perfectly with the conception of art as appealing in three ways, to the senses,
to the emotions, and to the intellect. Moreover, the
theory and alignment here suggested are broad
enough to include the forms of theatre art that
very recently have been created, and that indubitably
are entitled to a place in any complete system of
dramatic æsthetics, though denied that place by the
old and generally-accepted systems.

There must come soon the general acceptance of
a theory of the theatre which differs radically from
those of yesterday. If the present essay to formulate the new basis does not escape entirely the faults
that were so noticeable in the outworn systems, at
least it should point the way to an ultimate clear-
ing of the field. But after all it is written not for
the æstheticians but for the drama-lover; and if he
finds in it some guide-posts that will make easier his
pleasant rambles in theatre-land, the philosophers
may take care of themselves.

*     *     *     *     *

There must be appended to this chapter of theory
brief explanations of certain terms whose meanings
have become confused through continual misuse.
Certain qualifying definitions are absolutely necessary for the complete understanding of the writer's
intention.

*Idealism* is a word dangerous to use, as often is

done, in contrast with realism or with any other term in æsthetics; because to deny the idealistic quality to a painting, or a statue, or a drama, is to deny to it that for which art exists. For all art is in its very nature idealistic. If the artist does not add to his material that something which makes it an improvement upon nature, he no longer is the creator, but merely a copyist, a slavish photographer. The dramatist may indeed choose his material from strata of life that we recognize as outwardly un-idealistic, but if it does not undergo a certain sort of idealization in the process of artistic transformation, it remains mere life or nature and never becomes true art.

*Realism* is the most abused word in the terminology of art. It is employed continually as a synonym of naturalism, and as an antonym of idealism and symbolism—as if the art world could be halved, the one part being clearly realistic, the other idealistic or symbolistic.

But the realist as much as the idealist strikes down to what is deeply characteristic, stripping nature of irrelevancies. Both show forth not the outward semblances of nature but the essences of life. Both are artist-interpreters. The realist may indeed be distinguished from the idealist in the sense that the one remains closer to man's actual experience, closer to what really happens to all of us, while the other strays into higher flights of imaginative experience.  One tends to the particular, the other to the general.  But one of the fine things about the new dramatists is that they have proved that the artist may seek more precise knowledge of the facts of life and still employ an ennobling idealism in interpreting that knowledge.  They have shown that there is idealism underlying the everyday world if only the artist's vision is wide enough and penetrating enough to find it; and that the hand of genius can uncover beauty in the common clay of life as well as in the stuff kings are made of.  The extreme idealist may be said to make more beautiful what already is beautiful, whereas the extreme realist brings beauty out of the commonplaceness or even ugliness of everyday life.

The only absolute distinction should be between realism, or idealism, and naturalism.

For *Naturalism* is merely the servile imitation of nature, and has nothing at all to do with art.  Although realism and idealism may go hand in hand, both are separated from naturalism by an unbridgeable gulf.  For while the artist, whether more realist or more idealist, has to do with the essence of life, the "naturalist" makes no distinction between what is deeply characteristic and what is merely accidental.  The realist and idealist reveal hidden beauties, but the follower of naturalism merely imitates nature photographically.

The commonest phase of naturalism in the theatre

exists in the stage-craft of David Belasco and Sir Herbert Tree and their followers. For here the first aim is a perfect imitation, that will appeal to the audiences not artistically but by its naturalness, by its absolute fidelity to nature, down to the last unimportant detail. The practicers of this sort of stage setting miscall it realism, but it clearly has nothing to do with art.

All art exists in symbols: for as soon as the artist gets away from "natural life" and expresses himself by means of the essential or characteristic parts thereof, he is making something stand for something more than itself—and that is *symbolism*. The symbolist, the man who instinctively shrinks from calling a spade a spade, is the very opposite of the naturalist; but the realist and the idealist, as artists, necessarily employ symbolism.

*Poetry*, which certain theorists have counted, with action, one of the two essential ingredients of drama, is merely that intangible something which the artist puts into his work, the revealed beauty, the magic by which he transfuses life into art. The old definition limited poetry to literature written in verse; but recently it has been recognized that the essence of poetry may be found in prose and even in the wordless arts. The poetry in a play can be measured only by the breadth and delicacy of the dramatist's vision. That it happens to be written in verse means simply that the artist has chosen to add the outward beauty of metrically-flowing language; and while there is indeed a certain fitness in the addition of this appeal in some forms of drama, the prose play or pantomime may have quite as deep poetic or spiritual qualities.

# XI

## GORDON CRAIG'S SERVICE TO THE THEATRE

# GORDON CRAIG'S SERVICE TO THE THEATRE

There are two great revolutionary figures in the history of the modern theatre: Henrik Ibsen and Gordon Craig. Both revolted against the stagnation into which the drama had lapsed in the second half of the nineteenth century; but while the one took up the old dramatic form, rid it of its artificialities, and breathed a new life and a new spirit into it, the other cast loose from all accepted traditions and conventions of the playhouse, and sailing uncharted seas, arrived finally at a form of drama absolutely independent of the time-honored theory and practice of the theatre. Ibsen is the great reformer, Craig the great secessionist.

Craig's departure from the accepted theatre was based upon an entirely new conception of the nature of the art of the playhouse. He accepted the standard definitions that stressed action as the essence of the art of the theatre and of drama. But he interpreted action as meaning movement. And it is movement that is the fundamental material of all

275

the new æsthetic forms of drama. The old conception of action had been of something accomplished on the stage, as story-development, without
regard to the decorative value of the moving figures.
Thus a new meaning had been read into the phrase
"dramatic action," so that it came to be considered
merely an inner growth, a cumulative building of
ideas, a tense series of character-episodes; and Ibsen
especially had carried his art into a region where
the dramatic interest was entirely in changes of feeling and thought, where physical movement had no
part. Craig, arguing from the fact that the theatre
was primarily a place for seeing, concluded that contemporary drama was travelling directly away from
the true art of the theatre. He conceived of a new
art that would be typically theatric—that is, visually
effective—with its primary appeal that of decorative
movement. As he reviewed the points at which
men had approached such an art, in certain forms
of dancing, in pageantry, and in pantomime, he saw
strange gleams of a new and radiant beauty that
might be brought into the theatre.

With these visions before him, he looked about
for the artists who might work with him in em-
bodying the new ideal. In his futile search for those
who might help through their comprehensive knowledge of the theatre, he discovered the second great
lack in contemporary drama: there were no true
artists of the theatre.

Not only were there no men who understood all the departments of theatre production, playwriting, stage setting, lighting, costuming, and acting, but the production never was conceived as a whole, being created a bit here and a bit there by this and that man of the producing staff. No matter how perfect and how potentially dramatic the play might be when it left the playwright's hands, the final production always was a thing of scattered effect, in which distracting detail and accidental effect destroyed all spiritual truth and directness and sustained mood. For between the writing and the first performance a dozen artists and workmen had had hands in the making: the actor, the scene-painter, the costumer, the electrician, the carpenter, the manager—each had done his work without regard to the others or to the unity of the whole. Thus, while the contemporary playwright cared only for literary beauty or commercial success, the scene painter cared only to make his work attractive in itself, with an independent sort of effectiveness, forgetting that it should be nothing more than a background for the action; and the actor cared less for the beauty and dramatic quality of the play than that it should be a good vehicle for the exhibition of his own individual acting; and finally, the manager, who really should be able intelligently to direct the whole production, was only a business man who of necessity delegated his duties to a dozen incompetent assistants. So the production lacked the essential unity and sense of design that are at the base of all art. Moreover all efforts to reform the theatre had failed, because invariably they were directed toward only one part of the complex art of production. The real trouble lay in the fact that there were no true directors, no understanding artists who would be to the art of the theatre what the painter is to painting and the architect to architecture—the man at once of prevision and of execution. So there came Gordon Craig's plea for the new artist of the theatre.

The artist of the theatre will be a man who has had experience and training as playwright, as actor, as scene designer, as electrician, as manager—indeed in every department of the playhouse. Understanding thus every detail of his materials, and directing everything, he will be able to conceive, plan and carry out the entire production. Only when the production is thus entirely conceived and directed by one man, will it be a matter of *vision*—of imagination and unified design, as every true work of art must be.

The two ideas so far brought out form the foundation on which the whole of Craig's service to the theatre is built, and it is worth while to lay special stress upon them before taking up his actual experiments. First there is the new conception of the theatre production as primarily a decorative art, as dependent first upon beautiful movement, as something visually effective rather than emotionally stirring or intellectually interesting; and second there is the idea of totality of conception, the insistence upon the planning and execution of the production as a whole, and under the personal direction of a creative and all-understanding artist. The two fundamental ideas underlie the entire structure of the new æsthetic theatre, as well as the fast-spreading wave of reform in staging in the older psychologic theatre.

When Gordon Craig began to seek the laws that would govern the new decorative drama, that he visualized as a thing of unity and harmony and sustained mood, creative rather than imitative or interpretative, imaginative and symbolic rather than realistic or naturalistic, he already was fitted by heredity and experience to speak authoritatively of matters of the playhouse. For he is a son of Ellen Terry, the greatest English-speaking actress of her time, and of E. W. Godwin, an architect who designed the costumes and stage settings for many of the finest productions of his day. Gordon Craig himself was an actor for many years, appearing first when a boy of sixteen, with Henry Irving. So his first quarrel with the art of the stage was born of experience and not theory. He studied pictorial art, with William Nicholson among others, and developed the wonderful sense of composition and the dramatic simplicity which distinguish his very individual designs and wood-cuts. Thus he combined from his training the knowledge of two things that had been strangely divorced: drama and art.

Craig's practical work in the theatre has consisted in his staging of a long series of plays, from the "Dido and Æneas" of 1900 to the recent remarkable production of "Hamlet" at the Moscow Art Theatre; and in his experiments with the forms of silent drama, and particularly with marionettes. He has worked slowly, as a student rather than a professional director. Considering the number of years during which he has worked his productions have been few; but each one has been planned and brought forth with infinite patience and care. After each one there have been more experimenting, more changing, discarding and rearranging. Even now he does not feel that he has accomplished his ideal. But out of his incomplete achievement it is possible to trace three concrete attainments, of definite and far-reaching value to the theatres of the world. In the first place there is the creation of the new, and for many of us strange, art of the super-marionette; second the development of the mimo-drama of living actors, to which Craig gave the impulse rather than the embodiment; and third the reform of staging of the literary and psychologic dramas, the movement against naturalism in stage setting in the "regular" theatre. It is worth while to examine his achievement in each of the three directions of progress.

Let us take, to begin with, his pet form, his re-created puppet-theatre—so that we may immediately face his plans in the farthest limits of their radicalism; let us face squarely those ideas whose expression has drawn forth the epithets "Madness," "Revolutionary," and "Eccentric," from the very people who should by association be most concerned with the art of the theatre. It is worth while—without the hasty and unthinking criticism with which most students and commentators have approached the subject—to trace out in detail just what his art will be when planned and carried out in the ideal way.

Gordon Craig truly says that the materials of any art of the theatre are these: story or plot; movement; scenery; lighting; costume; the spoken word (if the artist wishes) ; music and dancing when woven integrally into the dramatic design; and the actor or the marionette.

The story may be little more than a bare skeleton on which to build: a bare plot or scenario. It must be simple and poetic rather than complex and realistic. Its effectiveness should come from imaginative beauty rather than from any compelling truth to life or deep emotional appeal. It should be lyric rather than epic or didactic; never should it attempt to carry an intellectual or moral message. This story, Craig admits, may be the work of another artist if it be thoroughly realized by the producer;

but it is even better if it be a creation of the director's own imagination.

The scenery or setting will be simple and unobtrusive. The artist of the theatre will not necessarily paint or construct it himself, but he will design it; and design it in such a way that it will be not a show in itself, but merely a background for the action, heightening the effect of the whole rather than distracting attention from it. It will be symbolic and decorative rather than historically accurate, attempting to reproduce "an atmosphere, not a locality." Perspective will be entirely eliminated from scenic backgrounds, because perspective on the stage invariably is distorted from all but one viewpoint in the auditorium; and furthermore, perspective lines serve to draw the eye out of the "picture." The principles of pictorial composition as applied to flat design will be applied to the setting, and the emotional value of certain lines and shapes will be realized to the full; as the majesty and profoundness of the long vertical, and the restfulness of the horizontal. Instead of the flapping wings and backcloths of the usual setting, Craig has evolved from his experiments a flat neutrally-tinted screen, made in various shapes and sizes, which is easily moved and adjusted. With a set of these screens he can arrange every setting called for in an imaginative drama, placing them in various relationships to gain the effects of spaciousness, severity, vastness, intimacy—in short, any *atmosphere* demanded by the *spirit* of the play.

Gordon Craig knows, better than anyone else perhaps, the emotional value of lights. The mood of the scene will invariably be suggested by the lighting, both in coloring and in the placing and movement of lights and shadows. He has discovered, too, that independent of any drama in the accepted sense, a whole story can be worked out by the interplay of colored lights on screens of various shapes and relationships. All his experiments in lighting, unlike those of others, have been purely for the beauty or suggestiveness of the resultant lights, and not to imitate nature. He can reproduce all of the beauty of moonlight, its essential spirit; but he never is guilty of trying to show a rising moon.

In the matter of costumes, too, imaginative beauty instead of naturalism will dictate the choice. The costumes will be simple and decorative, and like blocks of color in a great pattern—part of the color scheme and part of the decorative scheme. They will be true enough to the spirit of the time of the play not to be conspicuously unnatural, but not so painfully accurate that they will excite comment on their historical exactness.

Gordon Craig relies upon movement for the greater part of the appeal to the spectator. First there are the movements of the individual figures (whether actors or marionettes), that tell the story, since the new drama is wordless.  These actions and gestures will be simple, deliberate and infinitely expressive.  There will be no accidental tripping on a rug or falling over a chair to add a semblance of naturalness to the scene.  And since the story-interest is really secondary to the visual or decorative elements, the individual movement will be less important than the group movement.  Craig has shown for the first time the æsthetic value of the massing, grouping and interweaving of the figures on the stage.  Through harmony and rhythm of shifting figures he achieves a kaleidoscopic pattern of line and color.  The movement is in effect a continuous decorative pattern: a living mural decoration.  It is always and consciously under the control of the artist of the theatre.

The next point is that at which Craig departs from most of those who have followed him so far: he would leave the spoken word out of his materials.  Because strong feelings can better be suggested by gestures than by words, and because the spoken word is often an interruption of the mood, his ideal art is a drama of silence: the *mimo-drama*.  For the moment let us agree that in certain types of plays his claim is true, at least until we examine the final result; and let us accept for the moment his other most revolutionary doctrine; that the "über-marionette," or super-marionette, must ultimately take the place of the actor.  Because the living actor cannot subordinate his personality and temperament to the will of the artist; because his expression and his movement are always subject to his own emotions; and because the artist, on the other hand, must use only materials that respond absolutely to his will: therefore the marionette must take the place of the actor. Only thus can the artist of the theatre keep absolute control of the entire production.

Here, then, is a new art, different from any the world has known: an art of silent wooden figures, moving decoratively among beautiful colored lights and harmonious backgrounds, acting out a primitive, imaginative story. Its appeal is not at all the emotional or intellectual one of the usual theatre production, but is entirely sensuous. It is an appeal similar to that of music, which fails most completely when it tries to carry a didactic or intellectual message. The new art is æsthetic, imaginative, and suggestive, a thing of movement, color and rhythm, and of sustained mood, bringing to the spectator that deep soul-satisfaction described as "poetic wonder."

Who shall judge of the new art? Certainly the most of us, remembering the occasional moments of profound satisfaction experienced in the theatre of living action—imperfect though it may be—will not admit that Gordon Craig's creation is the *only* true art of the theatre. But who shall say that he is not developing an art that will play upon the heart-strings of future millions of theatre-goers even more sweetly than the current drama plays on ours? And who of us, soaked as we are in the traditions of a commercial or literary theatre, can judge fairly of this art that is so new, so foreign to all our stand-ards? Certainly it is an art wonderfully suggestive and beautiful. In the purity of its sensuous and imaginative appeal it is capable of evoking in the spectator something of that rapturous enjoyment that usually is a response to music alone. Indeed it is a thing that we should look forward to expect-antly and with every encouragement. And because it is truer to its own materials, and less dependent on literature, or painting, or music, it promises when completely developed to be the *truest* art of the theatre. Its effectiveness is in a way only provis-ional, since its audience has been a very limited one—but all those who have witnessed it in its finest accomplishment agree that it will be one of the most satisfying of the forms of drama.

It is not necessary to pause long over the second development that has grown out of Craig's experi-ments. For the mimo-drama, the wordless play of living action, is simply Craig's marionette drama with the human actor substituted for the wooden figure. The other elements are the same: the sim-ple imaginative story, the decorative movement that is more important than the subject-interest, the suggestive setting that unobtrusively heightens the mood, the decorative lighting. Max Reinhardt and those others who have brought the mimo-drama to its highest achievement followed Craig up to the point where he chose the wooden instead of the human actor. Sacrificing a certain abstract beauty—what Craig terms a "noble artificiality"—for a greater elasticity of movement and a wider range of expressiveness, they carried out Craig's ideal on a slightly divergent tangent. The effectiveness of the mimo-drama need not be argued here, since the discerning critics of two continents hailed "Sumurun," an example characteristically sensuous and decorative but rather too sensational, as affording a new and a joyous artistic experience.

How the Craig principles crept into the Continental Theatres and paved the way for the perfecting of the several forms of æsthetic drama, is clear when one considers that before 1905, when "The Art of the Theatre" first appeared (and was translated into German), Craig already had produced a number of plays in England and had at least made the designs for Berlin productions. Moreover his sketches and models had been exhibited in half a dozen European cities, and had stirred up a great deal of comment and discussion. It is to the credit of the Germans that they almost always give him credit as the originator and pioneer artist of the movement. Indeed it seems that in a very true sense Craig is not without honor save in his own country.

If Craig's service ended with his creation of the new æsthetic arts of the theatre, the world still would owe him a debt of gratitude. But of almost equal value is the influence he has exerted upon the accepted theatre, upon those arts that may be termed the *psychologic drama* in contradistinction to the æsthetic drama. In creating his new art he chose to ignore all that the theatre had accomplished in several centuries, turning his back completely upon the old forms. He felt that the "successful" playwrights, managers, actors, and scene painters had become so soaked in the traditions of a bastard form of dramatic activity, that they could bring nothing of value to his new structure. He preferred to create out of the raw materials an art entirely new —sweet, clean and beautiful—and not merely to accomplish a regeneration of the old form. His achievement is so fine that the world may easily forgive him for a certain intolerance in his attitude toward all but his chosen direction of work. But —and here is the important point to which almost all of his critics have been blind—he has exerted immense power over the very art which he so carefully ignored: the reform of staging that has resulted from the application to the psychologic drama of his principles of simplicity and suggestion and decorative beauty in setting is at least an equal half of his service to the theatre.

This other art of the theatre includes all those forms of drama which depend primarily upon story-development or character-development through dialogue. Its most typical and intensive form is the art of Ibsen and of Galsworthy, and it ranges from that to the extensive and literary drama of Shakespeare, from the more typically dramatic "Othello" to those many plays that are really literature thrown into dialogue form. It is clearly a legitimate art of the theatre, and true to the materials of the theatre. Contrary to the suggestion in Craig's attitude, the use of words does not necessarily put it into the category of literature: it is essentially drama, based on living action. The difference is merely one of emphasis on material: in the æsthetic drama the visual and decorative elements are emphasized; in the psychologic character growth and story-development are stressed, appealing to the emotions, and through them to the intellect, rather than to the senses. In the hands of a real artist of the theatre either form can be moulded into a unified harmonious whole.

The psychologic drama is not hopelessly bound up in false traditions. The art is very defective as yet, is very often given to cheap realism, false themes, and theatricality. But the leaven is working, and by a peculiar irony the leaven chiefly of

Gordon Craig's own ideas.  Let us see, then, what is his service to the psychologic theatre—what are the changes in each department of production that are following his revolutionary discoveries.

His greatest service lies in the reaction he has started against naturalism in stage setting.  The stage "artists" of to-day have indeed come to a wonderful perfection of naturalism, of photographic detail in setting.  If we did not know that we were in a theatre, we might even accept some of their creations as the real thing, the material illusion is so complete.  But the fact is that we always do know that we are in the theatre; and so it happens that the scene is unnatural just to the extent of its straining after naturalness.  For, after all, art is a convention, selective rather than photographic, dealing with the characteristic rather than the accidental. A stage setting can be absolutely right only when it suggests the mood of the play, the spirit of the whole performance.  It is not right when it is made up of a dozen tawdry flapping wings and backcloths and sky-borders; nor is it right when it is a photographic reproduction of a hundred accidental material details, distracting the spectator's mind from the essence of the play.  Gordon Craig believes that it is right only when it expresses the mood and unobtrusively heightens the effect, by symbolism instead of naturalism, decoratively and harmoniously, as a background and not as a show in itself—and his

## GORDON CRAIG'S SCREEN SETTINGS

*Gordon Craig recently produced "Hamlet" at the Moscow Art Theatre, using a single set of folding screens in varying combinations for all the necessary settings. In this sort of staging everything possible is left to the imagination of the spectator; there is no detail to distract the attention from the action—merely a perfect manipulation of line and mass, and of mysterious lights and shadows, to create mood. Illusion is created by suggestion—the only method legitimate in the theatre.*

teaching is quite as applicable to the psychologic drama as to his own created art.

Invariably when a student of Gordon Craig's work has become half convinced of the soundness and truth of his theories of stage setting, and of their fitness for psychologic as well as æsthetic drama, the comment comes: "All this is well enough for the setting of imaginative plays, but what about those that call for scenes in modern interiors?" It is the most searching of all questions that must be faced by those who believe in Craig's fight against naturalism and at the same time believe in the psychologic drama. It is worth while to face it squarely. How are Craig's theories to be reconciled to the plays of Ibsen, of Pinero, of Galsworthy? Craig does not care to reconcile them. He is concerned only with the imaginative drama, with his back turned squarely upon the "realistic" drama, and especially upon those modern plays which call for "up-to-date" settings. But the principles he has evolved apply to that sort of play none the less, and there is in his work a salutary lesson for the setting of modern scenes.

There can be no objection to a setting being natural, if its naturalness is not one of haphazard or strained detail and out of key with the spirit of the play. But the natural setting should be expressive of tasteful everyday life, with the accidentals left out—not of a stage director's tastelessness. In the modern room on the stage simplicity should be the first concern of the designer.  The wall spaces should be kept as unbroken as possible, for just as in the æsthetic drama, the attention should be concentrated on the actors; they should stand out clearly against a background divided into a very few large masses. The room should be cleared, moreover, of two-thirds of the usual clutter of furniture and naturalistic properties; the average stage parlor suggests simple domesticity less than the crowded aspect of a second-hand furniture store or old curiosity shop.

With a few chairs, a table, and a picture, a designer with perfect taste can create by suggestion an atmosphere that the tasteless average stage "artist" cannot achieve with either three times or a hundred times the same number of objects.  By the shape of the rooms, the height of the ceiling, the combination of lines, the placing of the openings, and by the disposition of the furnishings, and by the lighting, a modern room can be made to suggest the spiritual mood of any scene: cheeriness, severity, majesty, intimacy, depression.  But it can be done only by simplicity, economy of means, reticence of touch, suggestion, concentration.  These average overcrowded interiors, these depressingly accurate revelations of the stage director's lack of taste, make one pray indeed for Craig's ideal artist of the theatre.  Restraint, simplicity and appropriateness cannot find their place in stage decoration until there is a generation of directors who know the value of these things in real life.

Craig's teaching is quite as applicable to the lighting of the regular production as to the scenery. Unlike the "Wizard of the Switchboard," he seeks only that the light shall be appropriate to the mood, or beautiful, not that it shall be natural or imitative. One of the first things he decided in his experiments was that footlights, casting ugly shadows, must be abolished. It is difficult to see why they have persisted so long, since they are not only unbeautiful but unnatural.

In the psychologic drama of the modern sort one cannot follow out Craig's theory that the costumes should be imaginative and like blocks of color in a pattern. But one might write a long and much-needed plea for the simple and becoming costume for modern stage scenes. The stage has so far degenerated to a parade-ground for the ultra-fashionable in dress, that Craig's books might be read with profit by many a star whose vanity has got the better of her reticence and taste.

In the production of the psychologic drama, it is clear that movement and grouping of the figures on the stage cannot have the decorative value that Craig would derive from them in the imaginative mimo-drama. But his plea for a consideration of movement as a factor in heightening dramatic effect is a needed protest against the aimless, restless action

of so many present-day actors.  Movement which is
properly designed and consciously directed is the
only sort that is of value in a play that is based on
the first principles of art.

As Gordon Craig's new art of the theatre is
wordless, developing its story by action and light,
one might suppose that he would carry no message
of value to the artist of the psychologic drama in
regard to the story or plot.  Yet he has performed
a service in showing what is truly dramatic material.  Fortunately his voice has been only one of
many in the effort to teach that the stage should not
fulfill the function of the lecture-platform or the
pulpit.  If direct instruction is an aim, the theatre
is better left alone.  That does not connote that
there is to be no *idea* back of the play.  There must
indeed be a tangible basis for the story or plot, an
idea or theme.  But it must be so woven into the
action that it will at no place express itself as a
direct statement.  The first mission of art is not to
teach the brain, but to stimulate the imagination, to
appeal to the senses and emotions, to evoke a mood
or feeling in the person receiving the impression.
It is true that every deep emotional stimulus carries
a corresponding stimulus to the intellect; and some
of us may feel that the art that thus adds an intellectual appeal to the sensuous and emotional ones is
more vital than that which leaves no food for after-
thought.  But the point that Craig's attitude makes

clearer is this: that the production is not art when it becomes preachy and didactic—for art can properly carry a message only through emotional experience. The drama may stimulate thought, as we have learned from Ibsen and other modern dramatists, but the audience never should be conscious that the characters are preaching. Craig has taught, moreover, that the story must deal with the characteristic beauty of life rather than with the accidental detail.

If Gordon Craig opposes the didactic play on the one hand, he is quite as vehement in his protest against the purely literary play on the other. If the teacher has his lecture platform, the literary man has the library, and either one is out of place in the theatre. What often is called the "poetic drama," the play whose appeal is purely one of fine writing, generally is quite useless as stage material. The true function of the theatre is something more than a mere interpretation of literature. After many experiments with Shakespeare's tragedies—even after his own triumphant production of "Hamlet" at the Art Theatre in Moscow, which the most skeptical called a success—Craig has come to the conclusion that these immortal works cannot be adequately produced on the stage. Every lover of literature can remember the whole-souled satisfaction of his first reading of Shakespeare's tragedies, and the pleasure of conjuring up out of the imagination the magic backgrounds for the various scenes. And then was there not a distinct sense of disappointment when he saw them acted amid artificial scenery on the stage? Craig is without doubt right when he argues that the Shakespearean tragedies are so great *as literature* that no artificial setting in the theatre ever can be adequate. If they could be presented in the Elizabethan manner before audiences trained to evoke the proper settings from the imagination, the performance might be worthy of the text. But Shakespeare's plays are distinctly unsuited to the conventions of the modern playhouse and not only are they not typically theatric, but usually they are not dramatic in the sense of being tensely gripping, cumulatively absorbing. With the exception of "Othello" and "Macbeth," in which the dramatic element does predominate, and "Hamlet," that is in plot-outline a very compelling melodrama, Shakespeare's works are pre-eminently literature and only secondarily drama. Craig joins all other critics in hailing Shakespeare as the incomparable literary artist, but truly points out that Shakespeare in the theatre usually is the poet out of place. The production may be enjoyable for a number of reasons: for its historic interest, for the character-interpretation of a great actor, for the wonderful incidental bits of poetry, for the occasional humorous scenes, for the remarkable beauty of phraseology, and lastly as bringing back to the spectator reminiscence of something that has become dear in association through reading.  How much our enjoyment of Shakespearean productions depends upon this latter reminiscent interest is clear when we reflect that we always feel that we must *read* the play before seeing it, if we happen not to know it well; and if we see a production without a preliminary reading, we often are confused and even bored, and certainly do not get the pleasure that is afforded to our better-posted neighbors.  In other words, the appeal is not typically theatric, that is, not in the *seeable* elements, nor typically dramatic, that is, in action swiftly developing to a crisis, but primarily in poetry and story grown dear to us by association.

Of course, the substitution of the marionette for the actor would be impossible in the psychologic drama.  For not only is human speech necessary to the unfolding of subtle relationships, but in character development the actor can give a forceful, living response to the intent of the playwright or artist that is impossible to the lifeless marionette.  The best actors *can* subordinate themselves absolutely to the will of the director in spite of Craig's claim to the contrary, and they can heighten the mood of the play, can interpret its spirit, as the wooden figure cannot.  Except in very large auditoriums, facial expression, properly directed, is a distinct asset in interpretation.  As a matter of fact Gordon Craig formerly considered the flesh-and-blood actor perfectly good dramatic timber, and he had much to say about the "star" system, about naturalism in expression, about repression in acting, and about the use of the voice. But these things have been said by others quite as clearly, and they need not be gone over here.

Gordon Craig's general influence on the psychologic drama has been—and will continue to be increasingly so—toward unity and beauty, and away from naturalism. He is the prophet of a new simplicity in stage-craft. In setting, in light, in movement, in story, he teaches that each needless thing, each unnecessary realistic detail (no matter how appealing in itself), is an interruption of the main action, of the sustained mood. The method that he indicates for the accomplishment of his ideal art, is also the only practical remedy for the ills of the psychologic drama—the training of artists of the theatre.

One who studies the subject sympathetically and without prejudice must believe that only those who are interested superficially and commercially in the theatre—and not in the theatre as an art—can fail to take Gordon Craig seriously; and of those who really try to understand his viewpoint and then turn to scoff, one can only feel that they are so permeated with the traditions of a false art of the theatre that they are blind to any innovation, no matter how noble, which does not square with their own prejudices.

There doubtless is cause for the misunderstanding which surrounds the core of Craig's work. His essays, through which his theories are chiefly known, are stimulating, illuminating and prophetic, opening up to the reader unimagined realms of thought and beauty. But his style is intensely personal, even cryptogrammic. His expression often is confusing, and his argument never is summed up as a whole. He states the ideal, though he often follows the most practical. And after all he is only a student—an experimentalist, with his investigations incomplete. Moreover, he continually is outgrowing his own older theories, and his revolutionary ideas of a year ago may not at all accord with his ideas of to-day. But one who is not hopelessly steeped in the traditions of the existing theatre may dig down through the mass of confusion and misunderstanding, and find the foundations of a new art as beautiful as any the theatre has known; may find, too, the first impulses to the most wholesome forces that are to-day at work in the older theatre. Imperfect as Craig's work is, still in that imperfection is bound up the movement most vital to the drama of to-day and of to-morrow.

Before concluding it is worth while to pause to clear up certain misconceptions that Craig's own over-statements have served to foster. Wide publicity has been given to his statement that actors should appear with masks. Many a commentator has held him up to public gaze in ridicule as the man who would revert to the old custom of covering the actors' faces with grotesquely modelled masks. But one has the key to Gordon Craig's thought when one reads his statement that Henry Irving's face was the most perfect mask he ever had seen. To make the face a mask, to blot out of it all trace of personal feeling or emotion, but to paint there every shade of expression demanded by the character impersonated—that is the work of the perfect actor. The mask Gordon Craig had in mind must be an artificial one for the temperamental actor; but for the actor whose every movement is part of a preconceived design—and "art arrives only by design" he truly says—the human face *is* the mask; behind it is hidden the actor's own personality; upon it are expressed only the feelings and emotions of "the part." The plea is hardly more than a protest against the actor who is continually parading his own idiosyncrasies and his own shapely legs: a plea for surrender of individual personality in favor of deliberate action and designed movement that can be directed by the artist of the theatre. Similarly one must soften the meaning of that statement of Eleanora Duse which Craig has quoted with such gusto: "To save the theatre, the theatre must be destroyed; the actors and actresses must all die of the plague. They make art impossible." It is very clear that Craig did not intend an utter and everlasting annihilation of the theatre; but in a very true sense the old artificial theatre is being destroyed —and he more than any other is helping to build a new. As for the actors all dying of the plague, he really is too soft-hearted to wish it either literally or metaphorically; for although his ideal new art as sketched in his writings is to be a drama of wooden figures, it is noticeable that in his actual productions the living body has a very important place. And he now says that he will be content in his experiments only when he can test all materials and all forms. Again it is the actor in his average modern embodiment, and not the *genus actor* that he has in mind. The third misconception about Craig is that he talks much about the art of the theatre but accomplishes little. Because he has preferred to go very slowly, testing and discarding and building anew (the "Hamlet" production in Moscow was three years in the making), he has been termed a mere dreamer. He is indeed the original thinker rather than the practitioner, primarily the prophet rather than the doer. In that he is like Tolstoy, who more than any other man started the wave of moral progress that is sweeping over the world, but who never accomplished a bit of practical reform work because he was so impatient of all organized effort and restraint. Nevertheless Craig has done some practical work, as the long list of his actual productions shows. And now that he has his school for students of the theatre endowed and actually started in Florence, we may expect to have many more artists of the theatre to carry on the good work.

Gordon Craig's service to the theatre is so various that a summary is difficult; but because his influence does exist in so many fields, the summing up of the theatre's debt to him is doubly necessary, that the final understanding may not be confused. His service lies in two general directions: first, in what is practically the creation of a new art of the theatre, the æsthetic drama, an impressionistic form in which a sweet exaltation comes to the spectator through the artist's decorative use of dramatic materials (without stress on spoken words and sometimes without living action); second, in influencing away from an unbeautiful naturalism that other legitimate form, the psychologic drama, the drama of character development and soul crises. In the creation of the new art his work is unfinished, but it is opening up to humanity undreamed of vistas of beauty, promising a glorious new satisfaction of man's desire for sensuous enjoyment. In his service to the psychologic drama he has started that wholesome reaction against a strained imitation and against distracting naturalism in setting, in lighting, in acting, that is the most vital movement in the "regular" theatre to-day. He brought into the theatre a new conception of production as one integral harmonious art. In his insistence on the unified building up of his new art he voiced a need quite as pressing for the other form—the need for artists of the theatre. The training of such artists is, indeed, his one great practical remedy for the evils of the playhouse. His service to the theatre through his writings is inestimable because, imperfect though his essays may be, they are instinct with revolutionary ideas, and stimulating to the imagination, invariably impregnating the reader's mind with the desire to create. His essays, experiments and exhibitions were the first source of inspiration to Hevesi, and Stanislavsky, and Max Reinhardt and to the several others who are doing pioneer work in the theatre of to-morrow. They are putting into practice, often timidly or blunderingly perhaps, those principles which Gordon Craig had hardly more than stated in theory. He is the prophet and they are the followers.

Such is the service of this man of art, this genius, who, like all prophets, was born into a generation which could not understand him. It is not to be expected that he would be accepted by those money-changers in the temple whose false order he is upsetting. But the new race of artists of the theatre, those men who will build this art anew upon the principles which underlie all the true arts, for all time to come will acknowledge him as the master.